Harvard
Business
Review

ON

INNOVATION

THE HARVARD BUSINESS REVIEW PAPERBACK SERIES

The series is designed to bring today's managers and professionals the fundamental information they need to stay competitive in a fast-moving world. From the preeminent thinkers whose work has defined an entire field to the rising stars who will redefine the way we think about business, here are the leading minds and landmark ideas that have established the *Harvard Business Review* as required reading for ambitious businesspeople in organizations around the globe.

Other books in the series:

Harvard Business Review Interviews with CEOs

Harvard Business Review on Brand Management

Harvard Business Review on Breakthrough Thinking

Harvard Business Review on Business and the Environment

Harvard Business Review on the Business Value of IT

Harvard Business Review on Change

Harvard Business Review on Corporate Governance

Harvard Business Review on Corporate Strategy

Harvard Business Review on Crisis Management

Harvard Business Review on Decision Making

Harvard Business Review on Effective Communication

Harvard Business Review on Entrepreneurship

Harvard Business Review on Finding and Keeping the Best People

Harvard Business Review on Knowledge Management

Harvard Business Review on Leadership

Harvard Business Review on Managing High-Tech Industries

Harvard Business Review on Managing People

Harvard Business Review on Managing Uncertainty

Harvard Business Review on Managing the Value Chain

Other books in the series (continued):

Harvard Business Review on Measuring Corporate Performance

Harvard Business Review on Mergers and Acquisitions

Harvard Business Review on Negotiation and Conflict Resolution

Harvard Business Review on Nonprofits

Harvard Business Review on Organizational Learning

Harvard Business Review on Strategies for Growth

Harvard Business Review on Work and Life Balance

Harvard Business Review

ON

INNOVATION

A HARVARD BUSINESS REVIEW PAPERBACK

The *Harvard Business Review* articles in this collection are available as individual reprints. Discounts apply to quantity purchases. For information and ordering, please contact Customer Service, Harvard Business School Publishing, Boston, MA 02163. Telephone: (617) 783-7500 or (800) 988-0886, 8 A.M. to 6 P.M. Eastern Time, Monday through Friday. Fax: (617) 783-7555, 24 hours a day. E-mail: custserv@hbsp.harvard.edu.

Library of Congress Cataloging-in-Publication Data
Harvard business review on innovation.
      p.   cm. — (Harvard business review paperback series)
      Includes index.
      ISBN 1-57851-614-5 (alk. paper)
      1. Organizational change. 2. Organizational effectiveness.
3. Technological innovations.   I. Title: On innovation.
II. Title: Innovation.   III. Harvard business review.   IV. Series.
HD58.8 .H3694 2001
658.4′06—dc21   2001016866
                                                       CIP

The paper used in this publication meets the requirements of the American National Standard for Permanence of Paper for Publications and Documents in Libraries and Archives Z39.48-1992.

Contents

Harvard Business Review

ON

INNOVATION

Creating New Market Space

W. CHAN KIM AND RENÉE MAUBORGNE

Executive Summary

MOST COMPANIES FOCUS on matching and beating their rivals. As a result, their strategies tend to take on similar dimensions. What ensues is a head-to-head competition based largely on incremental improvements in cost, quality, or both.

The authors have studied how innovative companies break free from the competitive pack by staking out fundamentally new market space—that is, by creating products or services for which there are no direct competitors. This path to value innovation requires a different competitive mind-set and systematic way of looking for opportunities.

Instead of looking *within* the conventional boundaries that define how an industry competes, managers can look methodically *across* them. By so doing, they can find unoccupied territory that represents real value innovation. Rather than looking at competitors within their own industry, for example, managers can ask why customers make the tradeoff between substitute products or services. Home Depot, for example, looked across the substitutes serving home improvement needs. Intuit looked across the substitutes available to individuals managing their personal finances. In both cases, powerful insights were derived from looking at familiar data from a new perspective.

Similar insights can be gleaned by looking across strategic groups within an industry; across buyer groups; across complementary product and service offerings; across the functional-emotional orientation of an industry; and even across time.

To help readers explore new market space systematically, the authors developed a tool, the value curve, that can be used to represent visually a range of value propositions.

COMPETING HEAD-TO-HEAD can be cutthroat, especially when markets are flat or growing slowly. Managers caught in this kind of competition almost universally say they dislike it and wish they could find a better alternative. They often know instinctively that innovation is the only way they can break free from the pack. But they simply don't know where to begin. Admonitions to develop more creative strategies or to think outside the box are rarely accompanied by practical advice.

For almost a decade, we have researched companies that have created such fundamentally new and superior value. We have looked for patterns in the way companies create new markets and re-create existing ones, and we have found six basic approaches. All come from looking at familiar data from a new perspective; none requires any special vision or foresight about the future.

Most companies focus on matching and beating their rivals, and as a result their strategies tend to converge along the same basic dimensions of competition. Such companies share an implicit set of beliefs about "how we compete in our industry or in our strategic group." They share a conventional wisdom about who their customers are and what they value, and about the scope of products and services their industry should be offering. The more that companies share this conventional wisdom about how they compete, the greater the competitive convergence. As rivals try to outdo one another, they end up competing solely on the basis of incremental improvements in cost or quality or both.

Creating new market space requires a different pattern of strategic thinking. Instead of looking within the accepted boundaries that define how we compete, managers can look systematically across them. By doing so, they can find unoccupied territory that represents a real breakthrough in value. This article will describe how companies can systematically pursue value innovation by looking across the conventionally defined boundaries of competition—across substitute industries, across strategic groups, across buyer groups, across complementary product and service offerings, across the functional-emotional orientation of an industry, and even across time.

Looking Across Substitute Industries

In the broadest sense, a company competes not only with the companies in its own industry but also with companies in those other industries that produce substitute products or services. In making every purchase decision, buyers implicitly weigh substitutes, often unconsciously. Going into town for dinner and a show? At some level, you've probably decided whether to drive, take the train, or call a taxi. The thought process is intuitive for individual consumers and industrial buyers alike.

For some reason, however, we often abandon this intuitive thinking when we become sellers. Rarely do sellers think consciously about how their customers make trade-offs across substitute industries. A shift in price, a change in model, even a new ad campaign can elicit a tremendous response from rivals within an industry, but the same actions in a substitute industry usually go unnoticed. Trade journals, trade shows, and consumer rating reports reinforce the vertical walls that stand between one industry and another. Often, however, the space between substitute industries provides opportunities for value innovation.

Consider Home Depot, the company that has revolutionized the do-it-yourself market in North America. In 20 years, Home Depot has become a $24 billion business, creating over 130,000 new jobs in more than 660 stores. By the end of the year 2000, the company expects to have over 1,100 stores in the Americas. Home Depot did not achieve that level of growth simply by taking market share away from other hardware stores; rather, it has created a new market of do-it-yourselfers out of ordinary home owners.

There are many explanations for Home Depot's success: its warehouse format, its relatively low-cost store locations, its knowledgeable service, its combination of large stores and low prices generating high volumes and economies of scale. But such explanations miss the more fundamental question: Where did Home Depot get its original insight into how to revolutionize and expand its market?

Home Depot looked at the existing industries serving home improvement needs. It saw that people had two choices: they could hire contractors, or they could buy tools and materials from a hardware store and do the work themselves. The key to Home Depot's original insight was understanding why buyers would choose one substitute over another. (It is essential here to keep the analysis at the industry, and not the company, level.)

Why do people hire a contractor? Surely not because they value having a stranger in their house who will charge them top dollar. Surely not because they enjoy taking time off from work to wait for the contractor to show up. In fact, professional contractors have only one decisive advantage: they have specialized know-how that the home owner lacks.

So executives at Home Depot have made it their mission to bolster the competence and confidence of customers whose expertise in home repair is limited. They recruit sales assistants with significant trade experience, often former carpenters or painters. These assistants are trained to walk customers through any project—installing kitchen cabinets, for example, or building a deck. In addition, Home Depot sponsors in-store clinics that teach customers such skills as electrical wiring, carpentry, and plumbing.

To understand the rest of the Home Depot formula, now consider the flip side: Why do people choose hardware stores over professional contractors? The most common answer would be to save money. Most people can do without the features that add cost to the typical hardware store. They don't need the city locations, the neighborly service, or the nice display shelves. So Home Depot has eliminated those costly features, employing a self-service warehouse format that lowers overhead and maintenance costs, generates economies of scale in purchasing, and minimizes stock-outs.

Essentially, Home Depot offers the expertise of professional home contractors at markedly lower prices than hardware stores. By delivering the decisive advantages of both substitute industries—and eliminating or reducing everything else—Home Depot has transformed enormous latent demand for home improvement into real demand.

Intuit, the company that changed the way individuals and small businesses manage their finances, also got its insight into value innovation by thinking about how customers make trade-offs across substitutes. Its Quicken software allows individuals to organize, understand, and manage their personal finances. Every household goes through the monthly drudgery of paying bills. Hence, in principle, personal financial software should be a big and broad market. Yet before Quicken, few people used software to automate this tedious and repetitive task. At the time of Quicken's release in 1984, the 42 existing software packages for personal finance had yet to crack the market.

Why? As Intuit founder Scott Cook recalls, "The greatest competitor we saw was not in the industry. It was the pencil. The pencil is a really tough and resilient substitute. Yet the entire industry had overlooked it."

Asking why buyers trade across substitutes led Intuit to an important insight: the pencil had two decisive advantages over computerized solutions—amazingly low cost and extreme simplicity of use. At prices of around

$300, existing software packages were too expensive. They were also hard to use, presenting intimidating interfaces full of accounting terminology.

Intuit focused on bringing out both the decisive advantages that the computer has over the pencil—speed and accuracy—and the decisive advantages that the pencil has over computers—simplicity of use and low price—and eliminated or reduced everything else. With its user-friendly interface that resembles the familiar checkbook, Quicken is far faster and more accurate than the pencil, yet almost as simple to use. Intuit eliminated the accounting jargon and all the sophisticated features that were part of the industry's conventional wisdom about "how we compete." It offered instead only the few basic functions that most customers use. Simplifying the software cut costs. Quicken retailed at about $90, a 70% price drop. Neither the pencil nor other software packages could compete with Quicken's divergent value curve. Quicken created breakthrough value and re-created the industry, and has expanded the market some 100-fold. (See the exhibit "Creating a New Value Curve.")

There is a further lesson to be drawn from the way Intuit thought about and looked across substitutes. In looking for other products or services that could perform the same function as its own, Intuit could have focused on private accounting firms that handle finances for individuals. But when there is more than one substitute, it is smart to explore the ones with the greatest volumes in usage as well as in dollar value. Framed that way, more Americans use pencils than accountants to manage their personal finances.

Many of the well-known success stories of the past decade have followed this path of looking across substitutes to create new markets. Consider Federal Express and United Parcel Service, which deliver mail at close to the speed of the telephone, and Southwest Airlines, which combines the speed of flying with the convenience of frequent departures and the low cost of driving. Note

---

Creating a New Value Curve

The value curve—a graphic depiction of the way a company or an industry configures its offering to customers—is a powerful tool for creating new market space. It is drawn by plotting the performance of the offering relative to other alternatives along the key success factors that define competition in the industry or category.

To identify those alternatives, Intuit, for example, looked within its own industry—software to manage personal finances—and it also looked across substitute products to understand why customers chose one over the other. The dominant substitute for software was the lowly pencil. The value curves for these two alternatives map out the existing competitive space.

The Value Curves in Personal Finance Before Quicken

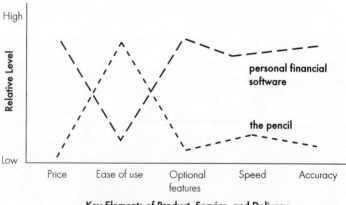

Key Elements of Product, Service, and Delivery

The software offered relatively high levels of speed and accuracy. But customers often chose the pencil because of its advantages in price and ease of use, and most customers never used the software's optional features, which added cost and complexity to the product.

that Southwest Airlines concentrated on driving as the relevant substitute, not other surface transportation such as buses, because only a minority of Americans travels long distances by bus.

The key to discovering a new value curve lies in asking four basic questions:

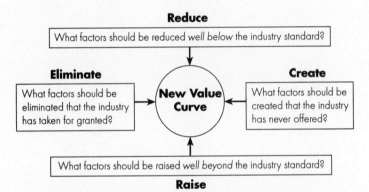

Reduce

What factors should be reduced *well below* the industry standard?

Eliminate

What factors should be eliminated that the industry has taken for granted?

New Value Curve

Create

What factors should be created that the industry has never offered?

What factors should be raised *well beyond* the industry standard?

Raise

Answering the four questions led Intuit to create a new value curve, which combines the low price and ease of use of the pencil with the speed and accuracy of traditional personal-financial software.

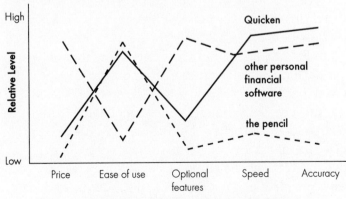

High

Quicken

other personal financial software

the pencil

Relative Level

Low

Price   Ease of use   Optional features   Speed   Accuracy

Key Elements of Product, Service, and Delivery

Looking Across Strategic Groups Within Industries

Just as new market space often can be found by looking across substitute industries, so can it be found by looking across *strategic groups*. The term refers to a group of companies within an industry that pursue a similar strategy. In most industries, all the fundamental strategic differences among industry players are captured by a small number of strategic groups.

Strategic groups can generally be ranked in a rough hierarchical order built on two dimensions, price and performance. Each jump in price tends to bring a corresponding jump in some dimension of performance. Most companies focus on improving their competitive position *within* a strategic group. The key to creating new market space across existing strategic groups is to understand what factors determine buyers' decisions to trade up or down from one group to another.

Consider Polo Ralph Lauren, which created an entirely new and paradoxical market in clothing: high fashion with no fashion. With worldwide retail sales exceeding $5 billion, Ralph Lauren is the first American design house to successfully take its brand worldwide.

At Polo Ralph Lauren's inception more than 30 years ago, fashion industry experts of almost every stripe criticized the company. Where, they asked, was the fashion? Lacking creativity in design, how could Ralph Lauren charge such high prices? Yet the same people who criticized the company bought its clothes, as did affluent people everywhere. Lauren's lack of fashion was its greatest strength. Ralph Lauren built on the decisive advantages of the two strategic groups that dominated the high-end clothing market—designer haute couture and the higher-volume, but lower-priced, classical lines of Burberry's, Brooks Brothers, Aquascutum, and the like.

What makes people trade either up or down between haute couture and the classic lines? Most customers don't trade up to haute couture to get frivolous fashions that are rapidly outdated. Nor do they enjoy paying ridiculous prices that can reach $500 for a T-shirt. They buy haute couture for the emotional value of wearing an exclusive designer's name, a name that says, "I am different; I appreciate the finer things in life." They also value the wonderfully luxurious feel of the materials and the fine craftsmanship of the garments.

The trendy designs the fashion houses work so hard to create are, ironically, the major drawback of haute couture for most high-end customers, few of whom have the sophistication or the bodies to wear such original clothing. Conversely, customers who trade down for classic lines over haute couture want to buy garments of lasting quality that justifies high prices.

Ralph Lauren has built its brand in the space between these two strategic groups, but it didn't do so by taking the average of the groups' differences. Instead, Lauren captured the advantages of trading both up and down. Its designer name, the elegance of its stores, and the luxury of its materials capture what most customers value in haute couture; its updated classical look and price capture the best of the classical lines. By combining the most attractive factors of both groups, and eliminating or reducing everything else, Polo Ralph Lauren not only captured share from both segments but also drew many new customers into the market.

Many companies have found new market space by looking across strategic groups. In the luxury car market, Toyota's Lexus carved out a new space by offering the quality of the high-end Mercedes, BMW, and Jaguar at a price closer to the lower-end Cadillac and Lincoln. And think of the Sony Walkman. By combining the acoustics and the "cool" image of boom boxes with the low price and the convenient size and weight of transistor radios, Sony created the personal portable-stereo market in the late 1970s. The Walkman took share from these two strategic groups. In addition, its quantum leap in value drew into the market new customers like joggers and commuters.

Michigan-based Champion Enterprises found a similar opportunity by looking across two strategic groups in the housing industry: makers of prefabricated housing and on-site developers. Prefabricated houses are cheap and quick to build, but they are also dismally standardized and project an image of low quality. Houses built by developers on-site offer variety and an image of high quality but are dramatically more expensive and take longer to build.

Champion created new market space by offering the decisive advantages of both strategic groups. Its prefabricated houses are quick to build and benefit from tremendous economies of scale and lower costs, but Champion also allows buyers to choose such high-end options as fireplaces, skylights, and even vaulted ceilings. In essence, Champion has changed the definition of prefabricated housing. As a result, far more lower-to-middle-income consumers have become interested in purchasing prefabricated housing rather than renting or buying an apartment, and even some affluent people are being drawn into the market.

Looking Across the Chain of Buyers

In most industries, competitors converge around a common definition of who the target customer is when in
reality there is a chain of "customers" who are directly or
indirectly involved in the buying decision. The *purchasers* who pay for the product or service may differ
from the actual *users*, and in some cases there are important *influencers*, as well. While these three groups may
overlap, they often differ.

When they do, they frequently hold different definitions of value. A corporate purchasing agent, for
example, may be more concerned with costs than the
corporate user, who is likely to be far more concerned
with ease of use. Likewise, a retailer may value a manufacturer's just-in-time stock-replenishment and innovative financing. But consumer purchasers, although
strongly influenced by the channel, do not value these
things.

Individual companies in an industry often target different customer segments—large versus small customers, for example. But an industry typically converges
on a single buyer group. The pharmaceutical industry,
for example, focuses overridingly on influencers—the
doctors. The office equipment industry focuses heavily
on purchasers—corporate purchasing departments. And
the clothing industry sells predominantly to users. Sometimes there is a strong economic rationale for this focus.
But often it is the result of industry practices that have
never been questioned.

Challenging an industry's conventional wisdom about
which buyer group to target can lead to the discovery of
new market space. By looking across buyer groups, companies can gain new insights into how to redesign their

value curves to focus on a previously overlooked set of customers.

Consider Bloomberg. In little over a decade, Bloomberg has become one of the largest and most profitable business-information providers in the world. Until Bloomberg's debut in the early 1980s, Reuters and Telerate dominated the on-line financial-information industry, providing news and prices in real time to the brokerage and investment community. The industry focused on purchasers—the IT managers—who valued standardized systems, which made their lives easier.

This made no sense to Bloomberg. Traders and analysts, not IT managers, make or lose millions of dollars for their employers each day. Profit opportunities come from disparities in information. When markets are active, traders and analysts must make rapid decisions. Every second counts.

So Bloomberg designed a system specifically to offer traders better value, one with easy-to-use terminals and keyboards labeled with familiar financial terms. The systems also have two flat-panel monitors, so traders can see all the information they need at once without having to open and close numerous windows. Since traders have to analyze information before they act, Bloomberg added a built-in analytic capability that works with the press of a button. Before, traders and analysts had to download data and use a pencil and calculator to perform important financial calculations. Now users can quickly run "what if" scenarios to compute returns on alternative investments, and they can perform longitudinal analyses of historical data.

By focusing on users, Bloomberg was also able to see the paradox of traders' and analysts' personal lives. They have tremendous income but work such long hours that they have little time to spend it. Realizing that markets have slow times during the day when little trading takes place, Bloomberg decided to add information and purchasing services aimed at enhancing traders' personal lives. Traders can buy items like flowers, clothing, and jewelry; make travel arrangements; get information about wines; or search through real estate listings.

By shifting its focus upstream from purchasers to users, Bloomberg created a value curve that was radically different from anything the industry had ever seen. The traders and analysts wielded their power within their firms to force IT managers to purchase Bloomberg terminals. Bloomberg did not simply win customers away from competitors—it grew the market. "We are in a business that need not be either-or," explains founder Mike Bloomberg. "Our customers can afford to have two products. Many of them take other financial news services and us because we offer uncommon value." (See the graph "Bloomberg's Value Curve at Its Debut.")

Philips Lighting Company, the North American division of the Dutch company Philips Electronics, recreated its industrial lighting business by shifting downstream from purchasers to influencers. Traditionally, the industry focused on corporate purchasing managers who bought on the basis of how much the lightbulbs cost and how long they lasted. Everyone in the industry competed head-to-head along those two dimensions.

By focusing on influencers, including CFOs and public relations people, Philips came to understand that the price and life of bulbs did not account for the full cost of lighting. Because lamps contained environmentally toxic mercury, companies faced high disposal costs at the end of a lamp's life. The purchasing department never saw those costs, but CFOs did. So in 1995, Philips introduced the Alto, an environmentally friendly bulb that it promotes to CFOs and to public relations people, using those influencers to drive sales. The Alto reduced customers' overall costs and garnered companies positive press for promoting environmental concerns. The new market Alto created has superior margins and is

---

Bloomberg's Value Curve at Its Debut

To establish its value curve, Bloomberg looked across the chain of buyers from the IT managers that had traditionally purchased financial information systems to the traders who used them. Its value innovation stemmed from a combination of creating new features—such as on-line analytic capabilities—that traders rather than IT managers value and raising ease of use by an order of magnitude.

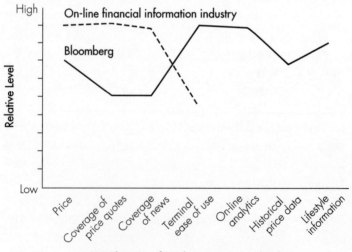

Key Elements of Product, Service, and Delivery

growing rapidly; the product has already replaced more than 25% of traditional T-12 fluorescent lamps used in stores, schools, and office buildings in the United States.

Many industries afford similar opportunities to create new market space. By questioning conventional definitions of who can and should be the target customer, companies can often see fundamentally new ways to create value.

Looking Across Complementary Product and Service Offerings

Few products and services are used in a vacuum; in most cases, other products and services affect their value. But in most industries, rivals converge within the bounds of their industry's product and service offerings. Take movie theaters as an example. The ease and cost of getting a babysitter and parking the car affect the perceived value of going to the movies, although these complementary services are beyond the bounds of the movie theater industry as it has been traditionally defined. Few cinema operators worry about how hard or costly it is for people to get babysitters. But they should, because it affects demand for their business.

Untapped value is often hidden in complementary products and services. The key is to define the total solution buyers seek when they choose a product or service. A simple way to do so is to think about what happens before, during, and after your product is used. Babysitting and parking the car are needed before going to the movies. Operating and application software are used along with computer hardware. In the airline industry, ground transportation is used after the flight but is clearly part of what the customer needs to travel from one place to another.

Companies can create new market space by zeroing in on the complements that detract from the value of their own product or service. Look at Borders Books & Music and Barnes & Noble in the United States. By the late 1980s, the U.S. retail-book industry appeared to be in decline. Americans were reading less and less. The large chains of mall bookstores were engaged in intense competition, and the small, independent bookstore appeared to be an endangered species.

Against this backdrop, Borders and B&N created a new format—book superstores—and woke up an entire industry. When either company enters a market, the overall consumption of books often increases by more than 50%.

The traditional business of a bookstore had been narrowly defined as selling books. People came, they bought, they left. Borders and B&N, however, thought more broadly about the total experience people seek when they buy books—and what they focused on was the joy of lifelong learning and discovery. Yes, that involves the physical purchase of books. But it also includes related activities: searching and hunting, evaluating potential purchases, and actually sampling books.

Traditional retail-book chains imposed tremendous inefficiencies and inconveniences on consumers. Their staffs were generally trained as cashiers and stock clerks; few could help customers find the right book. In small stores, selection was limited, frustrating the search for an exciting title. People who hadn't read a good book review recently or picked up a recommendation from a friend would be unlikely to patronize these bookstores. As a rule, the stores discouraged browsing, forcing customers to assume a large part of the risk in buying a book, since people would not know until after they bought it whether they would like it. As for consumption, that activity was supposed to occur at home. But as people's lives have become increasingly harried, home has become less likely to be a peaceful oasis where a person can enjoy a wonderful book.

Borders and B&N saw value trapped in these complementary activities. They hired staff with extensive knowledge of books to help customers make selections. Many staff members have college or even advanced degrees, and all are passionate book lovers. Furthermore, they're given a monthly book allowance, and they're actually encouraged to read whenever business is slow.

The superstores stock more than 150,000 titles, whereas the average bookstore contains around 20,000. The superstores are furnished with armchairs, reading tables, and sofas to encourage people not just to dip into a book or two but to read them through. Their coffee bars, classical music, and wide aisles invite people to linger comfortably. They stay open until 11 at night, offering a relaxing destination for an evening of quiet reading, not a quick shopping stop. (See the graph "Value Innovation in Book Retailing.")

Book superstores redefined the scope of the service they offer. They transformed the product from the book itself into the pleasure of reading and intellectual exploration. In less than six years, Borders and B&N have emerged as the two largest bookstore chains in the United States, with a total of more than 650 superstores between them.

We could cite many other examples of companies that have followed this path to creating new market space. Virgin Entertainment's stores combine CDs, videos, computer games, and stereo and audio equipment to satisfy buyers' complete entertainment needs. Dyson designs its vacuum cleaners to obliterate the costly and annoying activities of buying and changing vacuum cleaner bags. Zeneca's Salick cancer centers combine all the cancer treatments their patients might need under one roof so they don't have to go from one

---

Value Innovation in Book Retailing

Borders and Barnes & Noble looked across complementary products and services to establish a new value curve in book retailing. Their book superstores raised the selection of books, the level of staff knowledge, and the range of store hours well above the industry standards while lowering price and creating a wholly new reading environment.

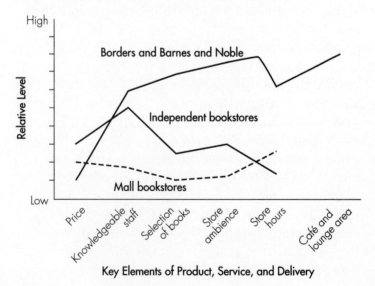

Key Elements of Product, Service, and Delivery

specialized center to another, making separate appointments for each service they require.

Looking Across Functional or Emotional Appeal to Buyers

Competition in an industry tends to converge not only around an accepted notion of the scope of its products and services but also around one of two possible bases of appeal. Some industries compete principally on price and function based largely on calculations of utility; their appeal is rational. Other industries compete largely on feelings; their appeal is emotional.

Yet the appeal of most products or services is rarely intrinsically one or the other. The phenomenon is a result of the way companies have competed in the past, which has unconsciously educated consumers on what to expect. Companies' behavior affects customers' expectations in a reinforcing cycle. Over time, functionally oriented industries become more functionally oriented; emotionally oriented industries become more emotionally oriented. No wonder market research rarely reveals new insights into what customers really want. Industries have trained customers in what to expect. When surveyed, they echo back: more of the same for less.

Companies often find new market space when they are willing to challenge the functional-emotional orientation of their industry. We have observed two common patterns. Emotionally oriented industries offer many extras that add price without enhancing functionality. Stripping those extras away may create a fundamentally simpler, lower-priced, lower-cost business model that customers would welcome. Conversely, functionally oriented industries can often infuse commodity products with new life by adding a dose of emotion—and in so doing, can stimulate new demand.

Look at how Starbucks transformed a functional product into an emotional one. In the late 1980s, General Foods, Nestlé, and Procter & Gamble dominated the U.S. coffee market. Consumers drank coffee as part of a daily routine. Coffee was considered a commodity industry, marked by heavy price-cutting and an ongoing battle for market share. The industry had taught customers to shop based on price, discount coupons, and brand names that are expensive for companies to build. The result was paper-thin profit margins and low growth.

Instead of viewing coffee as a functional product, Starbucks set out to make coffee an emotional experience, what customers often refer to as a "caffeine-induced oasis." The big three sold a commodity—coffee by the can; Starbucks sold a retailing concept—the coffee bar. The coffee bars offered a chic gathering place, status, relaxation, conversation, and creative coffee drinks. Starbucks turned coffee into an emotional experience and ordinary people into coffee connoisseurs for whom the steep $3-per-cup price seemed reasonable. With almost no advertising, Starbucks became a national brand with margins roughly five times the industry average.

What Starbucks did for coffee, Swatch did for budget watches. Long considered a functional item, budget watches were bought merely to keep track of time. Citizen and Seiko, the leaders in the industry, competed through advances in functionality by using quartz technology to improve accuracy, for example, or by making digital displays that were easier to read. Swatch turned budget watches into fashion accessories.

SMH, the Swiss parent company, created a design lab in Italy to turn its watches into a fashion statement, combining powerful technology with fantasy. "You wear a watch on your wrist, right against your skin," explains chairman Nicholas Hayek. "It can be an important part of your image. I believed that if we could add genuine emotion to the product and a strong message, we could succeed in dominating the industry and creating a powerful market." Before Swatch, people usually purchased only one watch. Swatch made repeat purchases the standard. In Italy, the average person owns six Swatches to fit their different moods and looks.

The Body Shop created new market space by shifting in the opposite direction, from an emotional appeal to a functional one. Few industries are more emotionally oriented than cosmetics. The industry sells glamour and beauty, hopes and dreams as much as it sells products. On average, packaging and advertising constitute 85% of cosmetics companies' costs.

By stripping away the emotional appeal, the Body Shop realized tremendous cost savings. Since customers get no practical value from the money the industry spends on packaging, the Body Shop uses simple refillable plastic bottles. The Body Shop spends little on advertising, again because its customers get no functional value from it. In short, the Body Shop hardly looks like a cosmetics company at all. The company's approach—and its emphasis on natural ingredients and healthy living—was so refreshingly simple that it won consumers over through common sense and created new market space in an industry accustomed to competing on a tried-and-true formula. (See the graph "Is the Body Shop a Cosmetics Company?")

A burst of new market creation is under way in a number of service industries that are following this pattern. Relationship businesses like insurance, banking, and investing have relied heavily on the emotional bond between broker and client. They are ripe for change. Direct Line Insurance in Britain, for example, has done away with traditional brokers. It reasoned that customers would not need the hand-holding and emotional comfort that brokers traditionally provide if the company did a better job of, for example, paying claims

---

Is the Body Shop a Cosmetics Company?

By reconsidering the traditional basis of appeal of its industry, the Body Shop created a value curve so divergent that it hardly looks like a cosmetics company at all. In appealing to function rather than emotion, the Body Shop reduced price, glamour, and packaging costs while creating a new emphasis on natural ingredients and healthy living.

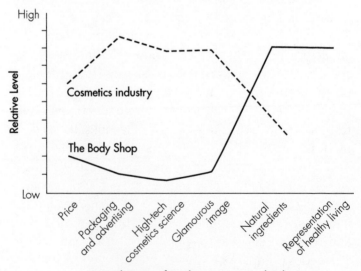

Key Elements of Product, Service, and Delivery

rapidly and eliminating complicated paperwork. So instead of using brokers and regional branch offices, Direct Line substitutes information technology to improve claims handling, and it passes on some of the cost savings to customers in the form of lower insurance premiums. In the United States, Vanguard Group in index funds and Charles Schwab in brokerage services are doing the same in the investment industry, creating new market space by transforming emotionally oriented businesses based on personal relationships into high-performance, low-cost functional businesses.

Looking Across Time

All industries are subject to external trends that affect their businesses over time. Think of the rapid rise of the Internet or the global movement toward protecting the environment. Looking at these trends with the right perspective can unlock innovation that creates new market space.

Most companies adapt incrementally and somewhat passively as events unfold. Whether it's the emergence of new technologies or major regulatory changes, managers tend to focus on projecting the trend itself. That is, they ask in which direction a technology will evolve, how it will be adopted, whether it will become scalable. They pace their own actions to keep up with the development of the trends they're tracking

But key insights into new market spaces rarely come from projecting the trend itself. Instead they arise from business insights into how the trend will change value to customers. By looking across time—from the value a market delivers today to the value it might deliver tomorrow—managers can actively shape their future and lay claim to new market space. Looking across time is perhaps more difficult than the previous approaches we've discussed, but it can be made subject to the same disciplined approach. We're not talking about predicting the future, which is inherently impossible. We're talking about finding insight in trends that are observable today. (See the diagram "Shifting the Focus of Strategy.")

Shifting the Focus of Strategy

From Head-to-Head Competition to Creating New Market Space

The Conventional Boundaries of Competition	Head-to-Head Competition	Creating New Market Space
Industry	focuses on rivals within its industry	looks across substitute industries
Strategic group	focuses on competitive position within strategic group	looks across strategic groups within its industry
Buyer group	focuses on better serving the buyer group	redefines the buyer group of the industry
Scope of product and service offerings	focuses on maximizing the value of product and service offerings within the bounds of its industry	looks across to complementary product and service offerings that go beyond the bounds of its industry
Functional-emotional orientation of an industry	focuses on improving price-performance in line with the functional-emotional orientation of its industry	rethinks the functional-emotional orientation of its industry
Time	focuses on adapting to external trends as they occur	participates in shaping external trends over time

Three principles are critical to assessing trends across time. To form the basis of a new value curve, these trends must be decisive to your business, they must be irreversible, and they must have a clear trajectory. Many trends can be observed at any one time—a discontinuity in technology, the rise of a new lifestyle, or a change in regulatory or social environments, for example. But usually only one or two will have a decisive impact on any particular business. And it may be possible to see a trend or major event without being able to predict its direction. In 1998, for example, the mounting Asian crisis was an important trend certain to have a big impact on financial services. But the direction that trend would take was impossible to predict—and therefore envisioning a new value curve that might result from it would have been a risky enterprise. In contrast, the euro is evolving along a constant trajectory as it replaces Europe's multiple currencies. This is a decisive, irreversible, and clearly developing trend upon which new market space might be created in financial services.

Having identified a trend of this nature, managers can then look across time and ask themselves what the market would look like if the trend were taken to its logical conclusion. Working back from that vision of a new value curve, they can then identify what must be changed today to unlock superior value for buyers.

Consider Enron, an energy company based in Houston, Texas. In the 1980s, Enron's business centered on gas pipelines. Deregulation of the gas industry was on the horizon. Such an event would certainly be decisive for Enron. The U.S. government had just deregulated the telecom and transportation industries, so a reversal in its intent to deregulate the gas industry was highly unlikely. Not only was the trend irreversible, its logical conclusion was also predictable—the end of price controls and the breakup of local gas monopolies. By assessing the gap between the market as it stood and the market as it was to be, Enron gained insight into how to create new market space.

When local gas monopolies were broken up, gas could be purchased from anywhere in the nation. At the time, the cost of gas varied dramatically from region to region. Gas was much more expensive, for example, in New York and Chicago than it was in Oregon and Idaho. Enron saw that deregulation would make possible a national market in which gas could be bought where it was cheap and sold where it was expensive. By examining how the gas market could operate with deregulation, Enron saw a way to unlock tremendous trapped value on a national scale.

Accordingly, Enron worked with government agencies to push for deregulation. It purchased regional gas-pipeline companies across the nation, tied them together, and created a national market for gas. That allowed Enron to buy the lowest cost gas from numerous sources across North America and to operate with the best spreads in the industry. Enron became the largest transporter of natural gas in North America, and its customers benefited from more reliable delivery and a drop in costs of as much as 40%.

Cisco Systems created a new market space in a similar way. It started with a decisive and irreversible trend that had a clear trajectory: the growing demand for high-speed data exchange. Cisco looked at the world as it was—and that world was hampered by slow data rates and incompatible computer networks. Demand was exploding as, among other factors, the number of Internet users doubled roughly every 100 days. So Cisco could clearly see that the problem would inevitably worsen. Cisco's routers, switches, and other networking devices were designed to create breakthrough value for customers, offering fast data exchanges in a seamless networking environment. Thus Cisco's insight is as much about value innovation as it is about technology. Today more than 80% of all traffic on the Internet flows through Cisco's products, and its margins in this new market space are in the 60% range.

Regenerating Large Companies

Creating new market space is critical not just for startups but also for the prosperity and survival of even the world's largest companies. Take Toyota as an example. Within three years of its launch in 1989, the Lexus accounted for nearly one-third of Toyota's operating profit while representing only 2% of its unit volume. Moreover, the Lexus boosted Toyota's brand image across its entire range of cars. Or think of Sony. The greatest contribution to Sony's profitable growth and its reputation in the last 20 years was the Walkman. Since its introduction in 1979, the Walkman has dominated the personal portable-stereo market, generating a huge positive spillover effect on Sony's other lines of business throughout the world.

Likewise, think of SMH. Its collection of watch companies ranges from Blancpain, whose watches retail for over $200,000, to Omega, the watch of astronauts, to midrange classics like Hamilton and Tissot to the sporty, chic watches of Longines and Rado. Yet it was the creation of the Swatch and the market of fun, fashionable watches that revitalized the entire Swiss watch industry and made SMH the darling of investors and customers the world over.

It is no wonder that corporate leaders throughout the world see market creation as a central strategic challenge to their organizations in the upcoming decade. They understand that in an overcrowded and demand-starved economy, profitable growth is not sustainable without creating, and re-creating, markets. That is what allows small companies to become big and what allows big companies to regenerate themselves.

Originally published in January–February 1999
Reprint 99105

Creating Breakthroughs at 3M

ERIC VON HIPPEL, STEFAN THOMKE, AND
MARY SONNACK

Executive Summary

MOST SENIOR MANAGERS want their product development teams to create breakthroughs—new products that
will allow their companies to grow rapidly and maintain
high margins. But more often they get incremental
improvements to existing products.

That's partly because companies must compete in the
short term. Searching for breakthroughs is expensive and
time consuming; line extensions can help the bottom line
immediately. In addition, developers simply don't know
how to achieve breakthroughs and there is usually no
system in place to guide them.

By the mid-1990s, the lack of such a system was a
problem even for an innovative company like 3M. Then
a project team in 3M's Medical-Surgical Markets Division became acquainted with a method for developing
breakthrough products: the *lead user process*.

31

The process is based on the fact that many commercially important products are initially thought of and even prototyped by "lead users"—companies, organizations, or individuals that are well ahead of market trends. Their needs are so far beyond those of the average user that lead users create innovations on their own that may later contribute to commercially attractive breakthroughs. The lead user process transforms the job of inventing breakthroughs into a systematic task of identifying lead users and learning from them.

The authors explain the process and how the 3M project team successfully navigated through it. In the end, the team proposed three major new product lines and a change in the division's strategy that has led to the development of breakthrough products. And now several more divisions are using the process to break away from incrementalism.

_____

Wʜᴇɴ ꜱᴇɴɪᴏʀ ᴍᴀɴᴀɢᴇʀꜱ ᴛʜɪɴᴋ of product development, they all dream of the same thing: a steady stream of breakthrough products—the kind that will enable their companies to grow rapidly and maintain high margins. And managers set ambitious goals to that end, demanding, for example, that a high percentage of sales come from products that did not exist a few years ago. Unfortunately, the development groups at many companies don't deliver the goods. Instead of breakthroughs, they produce mainly line extensions and incremental improvements to existing products and services. And as the pace of change accelerates in today's markets, that's a recipe for decline, not growth.

Given the imperative to grow, why can't product developers come up with breakthroughs more regularly? They fail primarily for two reasons. First, companies face strong incentives to focus on the short term. Put simply, although new products and services may be essential for future growth and profit, companies must first survive today to be around tomorrow. That necessity tends to focus companies strongly on making incremental improvements to keep sales up and current customers— as well as Wall Street analysts—happy. Second, developers simply don't know *how* to achieve breakthroughs, because there is usually no effective system in place to guide them and support their efforts.

The latter is a problem even for a company like 3M, long known for its successful innovations. Traditionally, the company's management has fostered innovation by taking a get-out-of-the-way attitude toward product developers who, in turn, have worked according to the aphorism "It's better to seek forgiveness than to ask for permission." This relationship between managers and developers has resulted in the creation of a long line of profitable products, from waterproof sandpaper and Scotch tape in the 1920s to Post-it Notes and Thinsulate in the 1970s.

But by the mid-1990s, 3M's top managers were concerned that too much of the company's growth was coming from changes to existing products. Breakthroughs were fewer and farther between. The demands for—and the rewards from—incremental improvements spurred the company to focus on current products. To counter this trend, management set a bold objective: 30% of sales would come from products that had not existed four years earlier.

For the company to meet that goal, many people at 3M—senior managers, marketers, product developers, scientists—would have to change their approach to their work. Accordingly, some employees started becoming acquainted with a new method for developing break-through products: the *lead user process*. The process—which makes the generation of breakthrough strategies, products, and services systematic—is based on two major findings by innovation researchers.

First, the researchers found that many commercially important products are initially thought of and even pro-totyped by users rather than manufacturers. (See the chart "Users as Innovators.") Second, they discovered that such products tend to be developed by "lead users"—companies, organizations, or individuals that are well ahead of market trends and have needs that go far beyond those of the average user. Those discoveries transformed the difficult job of creating breakthroughs from scratch into a systematic task of identifying lead users—companies or people that have already developed elements of commercially attractive breakthroughs—and learning from them.

Consider how an automobile manufacturer would apply the lead user process. If the company wanted to design an innovative braking system, it might start by trying to find out if any innovations had been developed by groups with a strong need for better brakes, such as auto racing teams. The automaker wouldn't stop there, however. Next it would look to a related but technologi-cally advanced field where people had an even greater need to stop quickly, such as aerospace. And, in fact, aerospace is where innovations such as antilock braking systems were first developed: military aircraft com-mands have a very high incentive to design ways to stop their very expensive vehicles before they run out of runway.

In September 1996, a product development team in 3M's Medical-Surgical Markets Division became one of the first groups in the company to test the merits of the lead user process. The team was charged with creating a breakthrough in the area of surgical drapes—the material that prevents infections from spreading during surgery. By November 1997, the team had come up with a proposal for three major new product lines as well as a new strategy that would take a revolutionary approach to treating infection. And the team may have done even more for 3M's long-term health: it persuaded senior managers that the lead user process could indeed systematize the company's development of breakthroughs.

But before we turn to that story, we must first explain how this process is different from other methods of product development.

Learning from Lead Users

All processes designed to generate ideas for products begin with information collected from users. What separates companies is the kind of information they collect and from whom they collect it.

Teams are usually taught to collect information from users at the center of their target market. They conduct focus groups and analyze sales data, reports from the field, customer complaints and requests, and so on. Then they rely on their own creative powers to brainstorm their way to new ideas. Teams that follow this method assume that the role of users is to provide information about what they need, and that the job of in-house developers is to use that information to create new product ideas.

The lead user process takes a fundamentally different approach. It was designed to collect information about

Users as Innovators

Research shows that many commercially important innovations are developed by product users rather than by the manufacturers that were first to bring them to market.

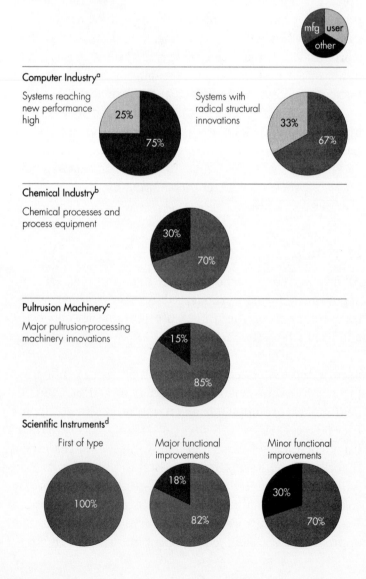

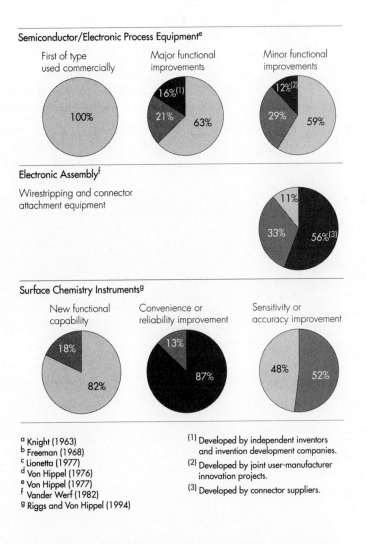

Semiconductor/Electronic Process Equipment[e]

First of type used commercially — 100%

Major functional improvements — 16%[1], 21%, 63%

Minor functional improvements — 12%[2], 29%, 59%

Electronic Assembly[f]

Wirestripping and connector attachment equipment — 11%, 33%, 56%[3]

Surface Chemistry Instruments[g]

New functional capability — 18%, 82%

Convenience or reliability improvement — 13%, 87%

Sensitivity or accuracy improvement — 48%, 52%

[a] Knight (1963)
[b] Freeman (1968)
[c] Lionetta (1977)
[d] Von Hippel (1976)
[e] Von Hippel (1977)
[f] Vander Werf (1982)
[g] Riggs and Von Hippel (1994)

[1] Developed by independent inventors and invention development companies.

[2] Developed by joint user-manufacturer innovation projects.

[3] Developed by connector suppliers.

both needs and solutions from the leading edges of a company's target market and from markets that face similar problems in a more extreme form. Development teams assume that savvy users outside the company have already generated innovations; their job is to track down especially promising lead users and adapt their ideas to the business's needs. (See "The Lead User Curve" for the shape of a market trend.)

True lead users are rare. To track them down most efficiently, project teams use telephone interviews to network their way into contact with experts on the leading edge of the target market. Networking is effective because people with a serious interest in any topic tend to know of others who know even more about the topic than they do—people who are further up on the "pyramid of expertise."

The Lead User Curve

The curve illustrates the shape of a market trend. Lead users have needs that are well ahead of the trend; over time, more and more people feel the same need.

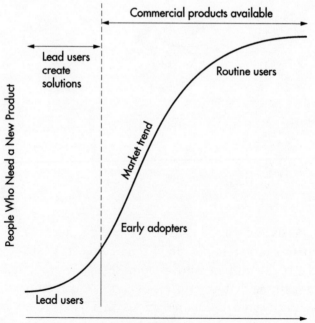

Team members begin by briefly explaining their problem to individuals who have apparent expertise on the subject—for example, research professionals in a field, or people who have written about the topic. They then ask for a referral to someone who has even more relevant knowledge. It's usually not long before a team reaches lead users at the front of the target market. The next step is to continue networking until lead users are found in markets and fields that face similar problems but in different and often more extreme forms. Those people can help teams discover truly novel solutions to important needs that are emerging in the target market.

Consider how a team focused on medical imaging carried out its work. Its members knew that a major trend in this field was the development of capabilities to detect smaller and smaller features—very early-stage tumors, for instance. The team networked to the leading edge of the target market and identified a few radiologists who were working on the most challenging medical-imaging problems. They discovered that some lead users among those researchers had developed imaging innovations that were ahead of commercially available products.

Team members then asked the radiologists for the names of people in any field who were even further ahead in *any* important aspect of imaging. The radiologists identified, among others, specialists in pattern recognition and people working on images that show the fine detail in semiconductor chips.

Lead users in the area of pattern recognition proved especially valuable to the team. Specialists in the military had long worked on computerized pattern recognition methods because military reconnaissance experts had a strong need to answer questions such as, "Is that a rock lying under that tree, or is it the tip of a ballistic missile?" These lead users had developed ways to enhance the resolution of the best images they could get by adapting pattern recognition software.

Lead users often help project teams improve their understanding of the nature of the breakthrough they are seeking. For example, the medical-imaging team's initial goal was to develop new ways to create better high-resolution images. But their discovery of the military specialists' use of pattern recognition led them to a new goal: to find enhanced methods for recognizing medically significant patterns in images, whether by better image resolution or by other means. (See the exhibit "Networking to Lead Users.")

It is rare for a manufacturer to simply adopt a lead user innovation "as is." Instead, a new product concept that suits a manufacturer's needs and market is most often based on information gained from a number of lead users and in-house developers. Some information is transferred in the course of telephone interviews or through on-site visits. More information is transferred when the team hosts a workshop that includes several lead users who have a range of expertise, as well as a number of people from within the company—product developers, marketing specialists, and manufacturing people.

A lead user workshop typically lasts two or three days. During that time, the assembled group combines its individual insights and experiences to design product concepts that precisely fit the sponsoring company's needs. In the medical-imaging example, lead users with a variety of experiences were brought together: people on the leading edge of medical imaging, people who were ahead of the trend with ultra-high-resolution images, and experts on pattern recognition. Together they created a solution that best suited the needs of the medical-imaging market and represented a breakthrough for the company. Executives at 3M charted a similar course.

Diving in the Deep End

In 1996 Rita Shor, a senior product specialist in 3M's Medical-Surgical Markets Division, heard an in-house lecture on the lead user process. Shor had been charged with developing a breakthrough product for the division's surgical drapes unit, and she needed help. Traditional market research was providing abundant data but could not point developers toward a breakthrough.

Networking to Lead Users

Project teams network their way up "pyramids of expertise" to identify lead users and experts, first in the target market and then in other key fields. The medical imaging team began by finding expert medical radiologists, who referred them to specialists in semiconductor imaging and pattern recognition. As a result of discussions with these lead users, the team's goal changed dramatically.

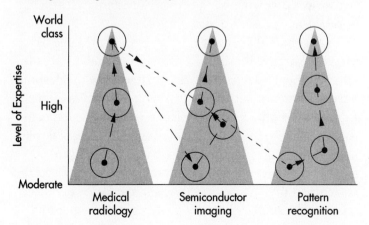

Shor called Mary Sonnack at 3M. Sonnack—sponsored by Chuck Harstad, 3M's vice president of corporate marketing, and William Coyne, senior vice president of R&D—had spent the 1994–1995 academic year studying the lead user process with Eric von Hippel at MIT. Shor put the problem to Sonnack in stark terms: "Our business unit has been going nowhere. We're number one in the surgical drapes market, but we're stagnating. We need to identify new customer needs. If we don't bring in radically new ways of looking for products, management may have little choice but to sell off the business." After warning Shor about the high level of commitment that would be needed from team members and from senior management, Sonnack agreed to work with her.

Surgical drapes are thin adhesive-backed plastic films that are adhered to a patient's skin at the site of surgical incision, prior to surgery. Surgeons cut directly through these films during an operation. Drapes isolate the area being operated on from most potential sources of infection—the rest of the patient's body, the operating table, and the members of the surgical team. But the diversity of the microbial world constantly challenged this protective fortress, which couldn't cover, for example, catheters or tubes being inserted into the patient.

By the mid-1990s, surgical drapes were bringing 3M's Medical-Surgical Markets Division more than $100 million in annual sales. But the unit in charge of the draping business had not had a breakthrough product in almost a decade. Technological excellence was not the issue. In the early 1990s, the division had spent three years developing technologically advanced disposable surgical gowns. The gowns would safeguard surgeons and their patients from dangerous viruses such as HIV—and keep them more comfortable—by allowing water vapor but not viruses to pass through microscopic pinholes in the fabric. This technological and manufacturing feat, however, came to the market just as managed health care was taking hold in the United States. Surgeons loved the fabric, but insurers wouldn't pay for it, and sales were disappointing.

In short, the division saw little room for growth in existing markets; declining margins on existing products; and, because of the drapes' cost, few opportunities to penetrate less-developed countries. Under those circumstances, Shor convinced senior management to try the lead user process. A few weeks later, she and her project coleader, Susan Hiestand, had assembled a team of six people from the R&D, marketing, and manufacturing departments. They all agreed to commit half their time to the project until it was completed.

Looking for Lead Users

The team's initial goal was, in essence, "Find a better type of disposable surgical draping." That was admittedly not a very creative first directive, but the way the problem is framed at the outset is not critical to the project's success. Experts and lead users are never shy about suggesting better ideas, and the evolutionary improvement of goals is an expected and desirable part of the lead user process.

The group spent the first month and a half of the project learning more about the cause and prevention of infections by researching the literature and by interviewing experts in the field. The group then held a workshop with management in which they discussed all that they had learned and set parameters for acceptable types of breakthrough products. (This work constituted the first

phase of the lead user process; see "Step by Step Through
the Process" at the end of this article.)

For the next six weeks or so, team members focused
on getting a better understanding of important trends in
infection control. One cannot specify what the leading
edge of a target market might be without first understanding the major trends in the heart of that market.

Much of the team's research at this early stage was
directed at understanding what doctors in developed
countries might need. But as the group's members asked
more and more questions and talked to more and more
experts, they realized they didn't know enough about the
needs of surgeons and hospitals in developing countries,
where infectious diseases are still major killers. The team
broke up into pairs and traveled to hospitals in Malaysia,
Indonesia, Korea, and India. They learned how people in
less than ideal environments attempt to keep infections
from spreading in the operating room. They especially
noted how some surgeons combat infection by using
cheap antibiotics as a substitute for disposable drapes
and other, more expensive measures.

As a result of their field observations, the team concluded that a crisis was germinating in the surgical
wards of developing countries. Doctors' reliance on
cheap antibiotics to prevent the spread of infection
would not work in the long run—bacteria would become
resistant to the drugs. The team also realized that even if
3M could radically cut the cost of surgical drapes, most
hospitals in developing countries simply would not be
able to afford them. Those insights led the team to redefine its goal: find a much cheaper and much more effective way to prevent infections from starting or spreading
that does not depend on antibiotics—or even on surgical
drapes.

The team members then networked their way into contact with innovators at the leading edge of the trend toward much cheaper, more effective infection control. As is usually the case, some of the most valuable lead users turned up in surprising places. For example, the team learned that specialists at some leading veterinary hospitals were able to keep infection rates very low despite facing difficult conditions and cost constraints. As one of the country's foremost veterinary surgeons explained to them, "Our patients are covered with hair, they don't bathe, and they don't have medical insurance, so the infection controls that we use can't cost much." Another surprising source of ideas was Hollywood. One of the team members learned that makeup artists are experts in applying to the skin materials that don't irritate and that are easy to remove when no longer needed. Those attributes are very important to the design of infection control materials that will be applied to the skin.

As a final step in the project, the team invited several lead users to a two-and-a-half-day workshop. (As "Why Lead Users Will Talk to Your Company" at the end of this article makes clear, the lead users' reward for participating was purely intellectual; they all signed over to 3M any property rights that might result from the workshop.) The bold central question, which had come out of the team's research, was now this: "Can we find a revolutionary, low-cost approach to infection control?" The participants met for several hours at a time in small groups; the composition of the groups was then changed and the process continued. Some groups floundered for a while before pulling ideas together toward the end of their sessions. In others, extroverted people at first dominated the discussion; later, the introverts warmed up and began contributing. All the groups faced the challenge of navigating a sea of facts and trying to unite creative ideas with technical constraints.

In the end, the workshop generated concepts for six new product lines and a radical new general approach to infection control. The lead user team chose the three strongest product-line concepts to present to senior management. The first recommendation was for an economy line of surgical drapes. The drapes could be made with existing 3M technology and thus would not constitute a breakthrough product; nevertheless, they would be welcomed in the increasingly cost-conscious developed world.

The second recommendation was for a "skin doctor" line of handheld devices. These devices would eventually be able to do two things: layer antimicrobial substances onto a patient's skin during an operation and vacuum up blood and other liquids during surgery. The skin-doctor line could be developed from existing 3M technology and would offer surgeons an important new infection prevention tool.

The third new product proposal was for an "armor" line that would coat catheters and tubes with antimicrobial protection. These products could also be created with existing 3M technology, and they promised to open up major new market opportunities for 3M. The company had previously focused solely on products designed to prevent surface infections; the armor line would allow it to enter the $2 billion market aimed at controlling blood-borne, urinary tract, and respiratory infections.

Changing Strategy

As a project team learns from lead users, the questions and answers it develops often point toward the need for strategic change. Indeed, that's what happened at 3M. Besides unearthing concepts for new product lines, the team had identified a revolutionary approach to infection control—but developing the competences, products, and services that would bring that approach to market would require the division to change its strategy.

Until this point, the division had focused on products that were, in a sense, one size fits all. Every patient, regardless of the circumstances that brought him or her there, would get the same degree of infection prevention from the same basic drapes.

In the course of their research, the team members learned that some people entered the hospital with a greater risk of contracting infection—because they suffered from malnutrition, for example, or because they were diabetic. Doctors thus wanted a way of treating individual patients according to their needs through "upstream" containment of infections. In other words, they wanted to treat people before surgery in order to reduce their likelihood of contracting disease during an operation.

Should 3M move in that direction? The members of the project team debated the wisdom of proposing a strategic change to senior managers. According to one team member, "In thinking about challenging the entire business strategy, we were crossing boundaries. I think the lead user methodology had pushed us in that direction. It allowed us to gather and use information in a different way than we had before, and it also provided emotional support for change. Based on extensive research, we were suggesting a major change—but as a team. We didn't feel like lone rangers."

But not everyone on the team wanted to make this last recommendation. One member feared that senior management might reject all the team's proposals if they made such a recommendation. In the end, the team decided to make the case for strategic change and successfully persuaded senior management to go along with it. As a result, implementation of the new strategy is well under way. 3M has established a "discovery center" service to develop and diffuse the new approach to infection control. And the product lines needed to deploy it are being developed. Details about the most revolutionary product lines are proprietary, and we can't reveal them here. But senior management believes the new strategy will produce very positive and far-reaching bottom-line results for the Medical-Surgical Markets group.

Opening New Avenues

3M has now successfully tested the lead user method in eight of its 55 divisions. Support among divisional managers who have tested the method has been strong. For example, Roger Lacey, head of the company's Telecom Systems Division and an innovative experimenter with the lead user process, says "the method brings cross-functional teams into close working relationships with leading-edge customers and other sources of expertise." Support among project teams also is strong. Developers at 3M regard lead user projects as creative, challenging work and will often adopt a project role on an informal basis before being officially assigned to a team.

William Coyne, 3M's senior vice president of R&D, believes the lead user process is the systematic approach to generating breakthroughs that had been missing at 3M. "Corporate management is very enthusiastic about the process, and the line of 3M people interested in learning the method from Mary Sonnack's group [3M's

Lead User Process Center of Excellence] extends out her office door and around the block."

Does the lead user process always guarantee success? Of course not; nothing can. Things like inadequate corporate support and inadequately skilled teams can derail even the most promising project. Nor will the lead user process crowd out projects and processes aimed at developing incremental improvements. Obviously, incremental approaches still have major value. But by giving companies a systematic way of finding the people and organizations on the cutting edge—those who are so impatient and so much in need of the next big thing, they are willing to make it for themselves—the lead user method opens up new avenues. It takes teams and companies in directions they wouldn't have imagined during the day-to-day crush of business.

Step by Step Through the Process

THE LEAD USER PROCESS gets under way when a cross-disciplinary team is formed. Teams typically are composed of four to six people from marketing and technical departments; one member serves as project leader. Team members usually will spend 12 to 15 hours per week on the project for its duration. That high level of immersion fosters creative thought and sustains the project's momentum.

Lead user projects proceed through four phases. The length of each phase can vary quite a bit; the 3M team spent six months alone on phase 3, when it researched surgical conditions in developing countries through on-site visits. For planning purposes, a team should figure on four to six weeks for each phase and four to six months for the entire project.

Phase 1: Laying the foundation

During this initial period, the team identifies the markets it wants to target and the type and level of innovations desired by key stakeholders within the company. If the team's ultimate recommendations are to be credibly received, these stakeholders must be on board early.

Phase 2: Determining the trends

It's an axiom of the process that lead users are ahead of the trend. But what is the trend? To find out, the team must talk to experts in the field they are exploring—people who have a broad view of emerging technologies and leading-edge applications in the area being studied.

Phase 3: Identifying lead users

The team now begins a networking process to identify and learn from users at the leading edge of the target market and related markets. The group's members gather information that will help them identify especially promising innovations and ideas that might contribute to the development of breakthrough products. Based on what they learn, teams also begin to shape preliminary product ideas and to assess the business potential of these concepts and how they fit with company interests.

Phase 4: Developing the breakthroughs

The goal is to move the preliminary concepts toward completion. The team begins this phase by hosting a workshop with several lead users, a half-dozen in-house marketing and technical people, and the lead user team itself. Such workshops may last two or three days. During that time, the participants first work in small groups and then as a whole to design final concepts that precisely fit the company's needs.

After the workshop, the project team further hones the concepts, determines whether they fit the needs of target-market users, and eventually presents its recommendations to senior managers. By that point, its proposals will be supported by solid evidence that explains why customers would be willing to pay for the new products. Although the project team may now disband, at least one member should stay involved with any concepts that are chosen for commercialization. In that way, the rich body of knowledge that was collected during the process remains useful as the product or service families are developed and marketed.

Why Lead Users Will Talk to Your Company

LEAD USER INNOVATIONS generate some kind of competitive advantage. When this advantage is significant, innovating users won't want to share what they know with competing companies or with manufacturers that would sell their ideas to competitors. Yet, most lead users are quite willing to give detailed information to manufacturers, and are usually willing to do so for free. There are two basic reasons:

First, lead users with compelling information often are in other fields and industries and would feel no competitive effects from revealing what they've done. Those lead users are generally happy to share their knowledge.

Second, lead users develop innovations because they need to—not as a source of competitive advantage.

In those cases, they may want to transfer their ideas to a willing supplier.

For example, in a lead user study devoted to improving credit-reporting services, a team found that at least two major users of such services had developed advanced, on-line credit-reporting processes. One of the users regulated the service it had developed as a significant source of competitive advantage and refused to discuss any details with the team. The other, however, welcomed the team with open arms and fully revealed its system. As one manager said, "We only developed this in the first place because we desperately needed it—we would be happy if you developed a similar service we could buy."

It is always good practice for lead-user project teams to tell interviewees up front that their company may have a commercial interest in the ideas being discussed. When someone hesitates to talk about his or her ideas, the interview comes to an end. That frees up team members to move on to find other lead users who don't have such concerns.

Thousands of Innovators

INNOVATIVE PRODUCT USERS often far outnumber an individual company's product developers. For instance, many people believe that user-developed software products, such as Apache's Web server software, are better than commercially developed products, That's less surprising when you consider that more than a half million Web sites use Apache software and that thousands of users participate in developing and supporting it. That is many times the number of people a commercial software developer like Microsoft can afford to dedicate to server software development and support.

And consider video game development. Sony recently set up a Web site to support hackers who are interested in exploring and developing new types of games that could be played on the Sony PlayStation. It quickly attracted 10,000 participants, a number that vastly exceeds the number of in-house and contract developers creating games for the PlayStation. It's likely that, taken individually, in-house developers are technically more skilled than most user-developers. But the user-developer community mobilized by Sony is diverse in its skills and interests. In a recent *New York Times* interview, Phil Harrison, Sony's vice president of third-party R&D, said he thinks several of them will come up with "some radically new forms of creativity that will break the conventions holding back the business today."

Originally published in September–October 1999
Reprint 99510

Building an Innovation Factory

ANDREW HARGADON AND
ROBERT I. SUTTON

Executive Summary

NEW IDEAS are the precious currency of the new economy, but generating them doesn't have to be a mysterious process. The image of the lone genius inventing from scratch is a romantic fiction. Businesses that constantly innovate have systematized the production and testing of new ideas, and the system can be replicated by practically any organization.

The best innovators use old ideas as the raw materials for new ideas, a strategy the authors call *knowledge brokering*. The system for sustaining innovation is the *knowledge brokering cycle*, and the authors discuss its four parts.

The first is capturing good ideas from a wide variety of sources. The second is keeping those ideas alive by playing with them, discussing them, and using them. Imagining new uses for old ideas is the third part—some knowledge brokers encourage cross-pollination by creating physical layouts that allow, or even force, people to interact with one another. The fourth is turning promising concepts into real services, products, processes, or business models.

Companies can use all or part of the cycle. Large companies in particular desperately need to move ideas from one place to another. Some will want to build full-fledged consulting groups dedicated to internal knowledge brokering. Others can hire people who have faced problems similar to the companies' current problems. The most important lesson is that business leaders must change how they think about innovation, and they must change how their company cultures reflect that thinking.

A SK ANY CEO IN THE WORLD to write a top-five wish list, and we guarantee that "more ideas—better ideas!" will show up in some form. Most likely it'll be right at the top. CEOs know that ideas and innovation are the most precious currency in the new economy—and increasingly in the old economy as well. Without a constant flow of ideas, a business is condemned to obsolescence.

We've spent the last five years studying businesses that innovate constantly, and we have good news for business leaders. The best of these innovators have systematized the generation and testing of new ideas—and the system they've devised can be replicated practically anywhere, because it has everything to do with organization and attitude and very little to do with nurturing solitary genius.

We learned two big things. The first is that the best innovators systematically use old ideas as the raw materials for one new idea after another. We call their strategy *knowledge brokering*; companies that do it serve as intermediaries, or brokers, between otherwise disconnected pools of ideas. They use their in-between vantage point to spot old ideas that can be used in new places, new ways, and new combinations.

Taking an idea that's commonplace in one area and moving it to a context where it isn't common at all is not a new way to spark creativity, of course. The history of technological innovation is filled with examples. The steam engine, for one, was used in mines for 75 years before Robert Fulton thought deeply about the original innovation, wondered how it could be used to propel boats, and developed the first commercial steamboat. Nobody had done what Fulton had with that particular local, specific knowledge: he made the leap of applying it to the altogether different problem of powering boats and implemented it in a way that was accepted by the marketplace.

The companies we studied have found out how to make that leap again and again (which is the second big thing we learned). We call their approach the knowledge-brokering cycle. It's made up of four intertwined work practices: capturing good ideas, keeping ideas alive, imagining new uses for old ideas, and putting promising concepts to the test. We'll show how innovators execute this strategy and what other companies can learn from them about innovation.

The Knowledge-Brokering Cycle

We found systematic innovators in all kinds of settings. There were product design firms like IDEO Product Development, business model inventors like Idealab!, knowledge traders inside consulting firms, and brokers such as Hewlett-Packard's supply-chain consulting group working inside huge corporations. Their markets and settings were diverse, but their approaches were not. Indeed, the four intertwined processes we observed were remarkably alike across companies and industries.

CAPTURING GOOD IDEAS

The first step is to bring in promising ideas. Brokers— companies that innovate by engaging in knowledge brokering—tend to span multiple markets, industries, geographical locations, or business units. They keep seeing proven technologies, products, business practices, and business models, and they recognize that old ideas are their main source of new ideas—even when they are not sure how an old idea might help in the future. When brokers come across a promising idea, they don't just file it away. They play with it in their minds—and when possible with their hands—to figure out how and why it works, to learn what is good and bad about it, and to start spinning fantasies about new ways to use it.

Designers at IDEO, which is based in Palo Alto, California, seem obsessed with learning about materials and products they have no immediate use for. At lunch one day, we watched two engineers take apart the napkin container to look at the springs inside. Another time, we brought a new digital camera to a brainstorming session, and the meeting was delayed for ten minutes while engineers took apart our new toy to see how it was designed and manufactured. IDEO designers visit the local Ace Hardware store to see new products and remind themselves of old ideas, and they take field trips to places like the Barbie Hall of Fame, an airplane junkyard, and a competition where custom-built robots fight to the death.

Brokers capture even more ideas from doing focused work on specific problems, especially when studying new industries or visiting new locations. More than 100 years ago, Thomas Edison's instructions about how to start a new project were as follows: "First, study the present construction. Second, ask for all past experiences . . . study and read everything you can on the subject." (For more on Edison and his successors, see "The Original Innovation Factory" at the end of this article.) Invention factories like IDEO and Design Continuum in Boston do pretty much the same thing today when they're trying to come up with new designs. They collect related products and writings on those products, and—perhaps most important—they observe users.

When Design Continuum was hired to improve the tools and techniques used in knee surgery, its engineers went to a convention for surgeons where they had the doctors re-create the surgical process in a way that allowed the engineers to watch and talk with the surgeons.

One of the engineers described the scene: "We wanted to observe the procedures, so we had a cadaver lab, which was actually in a swank hotel. One room was the lecture room and the other held 12 cadavers. They had the room chilled down to 50 degrees, with the cadavers in there and a guard 24 hours a day making sure nobody accidentally walked in. We just wanted to see how doctors used the tools, the little blocks and stuff they use for doing the procedures."

The result? Designers noticed that surgeons had developed elaborate habits to make up for what one engineer described as the "missing third arm." This inspired them to develop a new surgical tool that allowed doctors to hold, rotate, and operate on the kneecap.

When Design Continuum was asked to develop an innovative kitchen faucet for a client that had been producing faucets and related products for decades, it undertook a massive benchmarking exercise in order to learn not just about kitchen faucet valves but also about valves used in automobiles, medical products, and toys. The final design, drawing on many of those ideas, was for a pullout faucet that housed an integrated filter and circuitry to track filter life. The faucet delighted the client, whose engineers had assumed, after many years in the business, that they knew everything there was to know about valves. As CEO Gian Zaccai put it, Design Continuum's strategy "frees you from the dogma of any one industry."

"To invent, you need a good imagination and a pile of junk."
—Thomas Edison

Brokers also scan for new ideas in more generalized ways, because such scanning may pay off on the next project or the one after that. Andersen Consulting's Center for Strategic Technology brings in executives from diverse industries to talk about ideas for products. Joe Carter, head of the center, explains, "We invite people whose job it is to worry about the future of their companies." Engineers at Boeing's Operations Technology Center keep ideas flowing by holding companywide technology forums. And members of HP's supply-chain consulting group participate in workshops like the Stanford Global Supply Chain Forum to learn about practices used in different industries and countries.

Brokers thus create massive collections of ideas; some will lead to innovations, some will not. The important thing is that they're there. Edison once said: "To invent, you need a good imagination and a pile of junk."

KEEPING IDEAS ALIVE

This second step is crucial because ideas can't be used if they are forgotten. Cognitive psychologists have shown that the biggest hurdle to solving problems often isn't ignorance; it's that people can't put their fingers on the necessary information at the right time, even if they've already learned it. Organizational memories are even tougher to maintain. Companies lose what they learn when people leave. Geographic distance, political squabbles, internal competition, and bad incentive systems may hinder the spread of ideas.

The product design firms we studied are particularly good at keeping ideas alive, in part because much of each company's stockpile of ideas is embedded in objects that designers can look at, touch, and play with (it's easier to search through an actual junk pile than a virtual one). IDEO has made a science of accumulating junk. Many designers put plastic parts, toys, prototypes, drawings, and sketches on display in their offices. One engineer, Dennis Boyle, has an amazingly eclectic assortment of items that he constantly talks about and brings to brainstorming meetings to inspire new designs. A few years ago, it included 23 battery-powered toy cars and robots, 13 plastic hotel keys collected during trips, a flashlight that goes on when the handle is squeezed, an industrial pump, 11 prototypes of a portable computer, 14 prototypes of a computer docking station, six computers in various stages of disassembly, 15 binders from past projects, a pile of disk drives, a collection of toothpaste tubes, a toy football with wings, a pair of ski goggles he designed, a Frisbee that flies underwater, and dozens of other products and parts. He portrays this collection as "a congealed process—three-dimensional snapshots of the ideas from previous projects."

But there's more to the story. Six IDEO offices in scattered locations have cabinets known as Tech Boxes in which designers have placed a shared treasury of over 400 materials and products: tiny batteries, switches, glow-in-the dark fabric, flexible circuit boards, electric motors, piezoelectric speakers and lights, holographic candy, single-piece hinges, a metal-plated walnut, a widget from the bottom of a Guinness can that's designed to produce a foamy head, commercial toothbrushes, plywood tubes, and flip-flops from Hawaii. It began as Boyle's collection of interesting ideas, but it became a status game as people at IDEO competed to contribute cool new stuff.

Just as Boyle's collection would be useless if he didn't constantly talk about the items and discuss how they might be used, the memories in the Tech Boxes would soon die if designers didn't constantly look at the stuff, play with it, and use it in their work. Each Tech Box is now maintained by a local curator and each piece is documented on IDEO's intranet. Designers can find out what each product or material is and who knows most about it inside and outside IDEO. Engineer Christine Kurjan, head curator of IDEO's Tech Boxes, hosts a weekly conference call with the local curators in which they talk about new additions and the uses to which items are being put in new projects.

It's harder to keep ideas alive when they're not embedded in tangible objects. The people who designed knowledge management systems for Andersen Consulting and McKinsey originally thought reports, PowerPoint presentations, and lists of best practices would be sufficient. They supposed that consultants would be able to solve problems just by reading through databases. But consultants have found that those systems are most useful as annotated yellow pages, helping them find out whom to talk to about how the knowledge was really used and might be used again. Perceiving a need to link consultants together rather than refer them to stored information, McKinsey created its Rapid Response Team, which promises to link—within 24 hours—any consultant facing a problem to others who might have useful knowledge. The team accomplishes this feat largely by knowing who knows what at McKinsey.

Spreading information about who knows what is a powerful way to keep ideas alive. Edison was renowned for his ability to remember how old ideas were used and by whom. The most respected people at IDEO are part pack rat (because they have great private collections of stuff), part librarian (because they know who knows what), and part Good Samaritan (because they go out of their way to share what they know and to help others).

IMAGINING NEW USES FOR OLD IDEAS

The third step in the cycle occurs when people recognize new uses for the ideas they've captured and kept alive. Often those applications are blindingly simple. When Edison's inventors were developing the light bulb, the experimental bulbs kept falling out of their fixtures. One day, a technician wondered whether the threaded cap that could be screwed down so tightly on a kerosene bottle would hold light bulbs in their sockets. He tried it, it worked, and the design hasn't changed since. Old ideas can become powerful solutions to new problems if brokers are skilled at seeing such analogies.

Design Continuum engineers used analogical thinking to develop an innovative pulsed lavage, a medical product for cleaning wounds with a flow of saline solution. The new design had to meet cleanliness and safety guidelines, and it had to be low-cost and disposable. In thinking about pulsed lavage, the engineers were reminded of battery-powered squirt guns. Once they'd seen the similarities between an emergency-room tool and a child's toy—similarities that would not have occurred to most observers—the engineers could incorporate the squirt gun's inexpensive electric pump and battery into a successful design for a new medical product.

Design Continuum went through a similar process when Reebok hired the company to design a product to compete with Nike's Air technology. The people at Design Continuum asked themselves whether they could make a shoe that reduced injuries by providing more support and a better fit. The Reebok Pump with an inflatable insert was their answer. It drew on ideas from inflatable splints, medical IV bags, and tiny pumps and valves used in diagnostic equipment.

An effective broker develops creative answers to hard problems because people within the organization talk a lot about their work and about who might help them do it better. Companywide gatherings, formal brainstorming sessions, and informal hallway conversations are just some of the venues where people share their problems and solutions.

Many brokers also use a physical layout that enables (perhaps "forces" is a better word) such interaction. At the Menlo Park Laboratory in New Jersey, all of Edison's inventors worked in a single large room where, as one put it, "we were all interested in what we were doing and what the others were doing." Bill Gross put his Internet start-up factory Idealab! in a 50,000-square-foot, one-story building in Pasadena, California. It has few walls, so that everyone is forced to run into everyone else. His office is in the center, with concentric circles around it. The innermost desks are for start-ups in the earliest phases, when new ideas and support from others are most crucial. As businesses grow, they move farther from the center. If they reach a critical mass of around 70 employees, as eToys and CarsDirect.com have, they leave the incubator for their own buildings.

"The real measure of success is the number of experiments that can be crowded into 24 hours."

—Thomas Edison

IDEO's studios are also laid out so that everyone sees and hears everyone else's design problems. We witnessed hundreds of unplanned interactions in which designers overheard nearby conversations, realized that they could help, and stopped whatever they were doing to make suggestions. One day we were sitting with engineers Larry Shubert and Roby Stancel, who were designing a device for an electric razor that would vacuum up cut hair. We were meeting at a table in front of Rickson Sun's workstation. He soon shut his sliding door to muffle the noise from our meeting, but he could still hear us. He emerged a few minutes later to say he'd once worked on a similar design problem: a vacuum system for carrying away fumes from a hot scalpel that cauter-

ized skin during surgery. Sun brought out samples of
tubing that might be used in the new design and a report
he had written about the kinds of plastic tubing available
from vendors. The encounter shows how having the right
attitude drives people to help each other solve problems.
Shubert commented, "Once Rickson realized he could
help us, he had to do it or he wouldn't be a good IDEO
designer." (For more on attitudes—and people—see
"The Right People, the Right Attitudes" at the end of this
article.)

PUTTING PROMISING CONCEPTS TO THE TEST

A good idea for a new product or business practice isn't
worth much by itself. It needs to be turned into something that can be tested and, if successful, integrated into
the rest of what a company does, makes, or sells. Quickly
turning an imaginative idea into a real service, product,
process, or business model is the final step in the brokering cycle. By "real" we mean concrete enough to be
tested; by "quickly" we mean early enough in the process
that mistakes can be caught and improvements made.
"The real measure of success," Edison said, "is the number of experiments that can be crowded into 24 hours."

Knowledge brokers are not the only businesses that
use prototypes, experiments, simulations, models, and
pilot programs to test and refine ideas. The difference is
that collecting and generating ideas, and testing them
quickly and well, are more than just some of the things
brokers do: they are the main things brokers do.

Brokers must be good at testing ideas, at judging
them on merit without letting politics or precedent get
in the way. Brokers' attitude toward ideas is usually

"Easy come, easy go." They treat ideas as inexpensive and easily replaceable playthings that they are supposed to enjoy, understand, push to the limit, break, and change in ways the ideas' inventors never imagined. If an idea seems to solve a current problem, they build on it. If an idea doesn't work out, they look for another. Brokers rarely keep trying to make something work in the face of evidence that it won't. They focus on finding the best ideas for solving problems, not on solutions they can claim glory for. We call it the nothing-is-invented-here attitude. It means they reach out—early and often—to anyone who might help them solve problems and test ideas. The more familiar not-invented-here syndrome— in which people, believing they know more than others in their field, reject all new ideas that are "not invented here"—is viewed by brokers as inefficient, arrogant, and ultimately fatal to innovation.

Almost immediately after thinking of a promising concept, a development team at a place like IDEO or Design Continuum builds a prototype, shows it to users, tests it, and improves it. The team then repeats the sequence over and over. Prototypes can be anything from crude gadgets to elaborate mock-ups. IDEO designers in the Boston office built a full-size foam model of an Amtrak train to test ideas about seating, layout, and signage. To make more refined prototypes, IDEO's machine shop uses computerized milling machines and other sophisticated tools. IDEO's machinists can take a rough sketch and quickly turn it into a working model.

Testing prototypes is a way of life at Idealab! as well. Idealab! companies often start as experiments that cost between $10,000 and $250,000. Often they are prototype Web sites, opened temporarily to find out how many people will visit and whether customers will buy the product or service offered. For example, Bill Gross had the idea of selling cars on-line—not just using the Internet to send customers to a dealer but selling cars directly, as Dell sells computers. Gross didn't spend a lot of time planning. Instead, he quickly assembled a group to try out the idea. Instead of creating a fancy Web site that could link dealers or handle a lot of traffic, the group built something simple that worked just well enough to test the idea. Gross hired a CEO for 90 days and told him his job was to sell one car. The plan was that if a customer ordered a car, Idealab! would buy the car from a dealer and resell it to the customer at about a $5,000 loss. On the first day, the test site got 1,000 hits and sold four cars. The experiment led to the founding of CarsDirect.com.

Putting a concept to the test doesn't just help determine if it has commercial value. The process also teaches brokers lessons they might be able to use later, even when an idea is a complete flop. Brokers remember failures in part so that they can help the more focused businesses they serve avoid making the same mistakes. At HP's supply-chain consulting group—known as SPaM, for Strategic Planning and Modeling—one engineer explained that she could be just as helpful to members of an HP division by telling them about what didn't work in other places—and why—as she could by telling them what did. And Gross claims he learns at least as much from business ideas that don't fly as from concepts that do.

Brokers also benefit from failures because, in learning about why an idea failed, they get hints about problems the idea might solve someday. Edison's laboratory had a contract to design a new telegraph cable that would span the Atlantic Ocean. One approach the engineers tried was insulating the wires with a carbon putty. The cable worked on the lab bench but short-circuited in water. They eventually figured out that it failed because water pressure transformed the putty from an insulator into a conductor. But when they tried the carbon putty again a few years later in another application, the result was an inexpensive, effective, and reliable microphone that helped make the telephone commercially feasible.

Building Your Own Knowledge Broker

Most of the examples in this article are drawn from stand-alone innovation factories, but any company can use part or all of the knowledge-brokering system. Large companies in particular desperately need to move ideas from one place to another. The larger a company gets, the harder it is for anyone to know what everyone is doing. The specialization and separation that help business units maintain focus also hamper communication. Internal competition magnifies the problem, because it encourages groups to hoard rather than share what they've learned. Knowledge brokers that build reputations as trusted third parties thrive in such places. They find new uses for what the company knows and help dispersed groups avoid reinventing the same wheels—and making the same mistakes—again and again.

Take Hewlett-Packard's SPaM group, formed about ten years ago to help optimize HP's often-convoluted supply chains. Partly because they were measured against one another, few divisions were eager to share information about successes or failures with any of the more than 150 other divisions. Enter SPaM, which was, in leader Corey Billington's words, politically neutral. SPaM used powerful modeling techniques to save its first clients millions of dollars. Each new project also taught SPaM what clients were doing right and wrong, so the group soon had more than modeling techniques to sell inside HP.

Or take the Optics Technology Center (OTC) at 3M, formed in the 1960s after 3M engineers developed a way to create tiny prisms on the surfaces of lenses for overhead projectors. Management believed the engineers were on to something bigger, so OTC was formed to discover ways to spread the technology, called microreplication, throughout 3M. It is now used in traffic lights, industrial grinders, mouse pads, and dozens of other 3M products. As was the case with SPaM, each project taught OTC engineers something new, often opening their eyes to uses they hadn't imagined.

Companies can put knowledge brokering to work in various ways. Some companies—especially large ones—will want to emulate HP and 3M by building full-fledged internal consulting groups dedicated to knowledge brokering. To get started, the companies should identify people who have important information that a substantial number of groups in the company don't have. Those people needn't be the world's biggest experts; they just have to be more knowledgeable than the groups they're going to help. (If they do their job well, they'll learn from each project, and before long they *will* be among the world's biggest experts.) Initially, the experts may need to make an effort to sell their ideas; 3M's OTC once built an entire pilot production line to show management that tape products with microreplication could be manufactured in adequate volumes using existing machines.

Other companies may not wish to develop full-scale, formal knowledge-brokering groups. As an alternative, a company can develop the habit of hiring people who have faced problems that are similar or analogous to problems the company faces. Hiring such people can be an efficient way to import fresh solutions. For example, the tiny stents that Guidant Corporation developed to prop open obstructed heart vessels don't appear to have anything in common with the planes and missiles that defense contractors develop. Yet Ginger Graham, president of the Vascular Intervention Group, tells us that engineers hired from NASA, Hughes, Lockheed, Ford Aerospace, Raychem, and General Dynamics have bolstered Guidant's efforts to design stents and other medical products by bringing in materials and design solutions that are new to the industry.

For still other companies or divisions, occasionally renting an outside broker can make sense. We are wary of companies that outsource all innovation, because doing so undermines an organization's ability to learn or to evaluate new ideas on its own. But when a business needs ideas in an unfamiliar field and a broker knows the field well, renting the broker can be a wise move. As HP's Billington says, "If someone wants to streamline their supply chain, they might learn great stuff from talking to the hundreds of people we have worked with inside and outside HP. But it is a lot faster and cheaper to work with us."

The most important lesson from all this is that business leaders must change how they think about innovation and must change how their company cultures reflect that thinking. Innovation can be bolstered anywhere if people are given opportunities and rewards for taking good ideas—as long as no laws are broken—from all sources inside or outside the company. The image of the lone genius inventing ideas from scratch is romantic and engaging, but it's a dangerous fiction. Innovation and creativity are far less mysterious than that image implies. They are a matter of taking developed ideas and applying them in new situations. If your company has the right connections and the right attitude, it works.

The Knowledge-Brokering Cycle

1. **Capturing good ideas**. Knowledge brokers scavenge constantly for promising ideas, sometimes in the unlikeliest places. They see old ideas as their primary raw material.

2. **Keeping ideas alive.** To remain useful, ideas must be passed around and toyed with. Effective brokers also keep ideas alive by spreading information on who knows what within the organization.

3. **Imagining new uses for old ideas.** This is where the innovations arise, where old ideas that have been captured and remembered are plugged into new contexts.

4. **Putting promising concepts to the test.** Testing shows whether an innovation has commercial potential. It also teaches brokers valuable lessons, even when an idea is a complete flop.

The Original Innovation Factory

THOMAS EDISON CULTIVATED HIS IMAGE as inventor-hero and lone genius, but his greatest creation may have been the invention factory itself. His Menlo Park, New Jersey, laboratory—the world's first dedicated R&D facility—demonstrated that a stream of promising ideas could be generated if a company was organized in the right way. Rather than focusing on one invention, one field of expertise, or one market, Edison created a setting—and ways of thinking and working—that enabled his inventors to move easily in and out of separate pools of knowledge, to keep learning new ideas, and to use ideas in novel situations.

A hallmark of Edison's inventions was that they used old ideas, materials, or objects in new ways. The phonograph blended elements from past work on telegraphs, telephones, and electric motors. And the lab's early work on telegraph cables later helped its engineers transform the telephone from a scratchy-sounding novelty into a commercial success. Edison built the laboratory for the "rapid and cheap development of an invention" and delivered on his promise of "a minor invention every ten days and a big thing every six months or so." In six years of operation, it generated more than 400 patents.

Modern invention factories are springing up everywhere today. Since its founding in 1978, IDEO has developed thousands of products—from the Palm V for 3Com to the Twist'n Go cup for Pepsi—in more than 40 industries. IDEO's work with companies in dissimilar fields—such as medical instruments, furniture, toys, and computers—gives the company a broad view of the latest technologies. Lessons from IDEO's diverse client base inspire many original designs. For example, a Chatty Cathy doll supplied the idea for a reliable, inexpensive motor used in a docking station for an Apple laptop computer.

Incubators for start-up firms are also invention factories—they just invent business models, not physical products. Bill Gross's Idealab! is the most renowned of these. His "Internet factory" in Pasadena, California, houses about 20 start-ups at any given time. The companies try to succeed on the Internet by entering diverse markets using a broad range of business models. Gross encourages "cross-pollination" among all the people in the building and is himself a skilled knowledge broker, spreading ideas from one group to another.

The Right People, The Right Attitudes

COMPANIES THAT SPECIALIZE IN INNOVATION hire people with varied skills, interests, and backgrounds. The product design firm Design Continuum, for example, has plenty of engineers on staff, but it also has anthropologists and English majors—even a theater designer. And some of its engineers moonlight as sculptors, carpenters, or rock musicians. We once went to a brainstorming session at IDEO where an engineer who'd grown up on a farm sketched a miniature version of a harvesting combine as a novel haircutting device for a major national salon chain.

Sometimes it's not people's backgrounds as much as their passionate interests that make the difference. Engineer Dennis Boyle's lifelong fascination with toys has helped him and others at IDEO design laptop computers for Apple, Dell, and NEC, handheld computers for Palm and Handspring, and hundreds of other products. "Toys have so many neat things to offer," Boyle says. "They're high volume, mass produced, often plastic, and very clever because they're so cheap. I especially love Japanese toys. We bring them out in brainstorming sessions and apply the ideas to computers or surgical skin staplers or whatever."

There's a lot of movement into and out of innovation factories. IDEO rehired several employees who, after working elsewhere, came back to apply knowledge they'd gained on the outside. When former IDEO engineer Walt Conti worked for filmmaker George Lucas at Industrial Light and Magic, he discovered that the movie industry wasn't using the sophisticated control systems and electromechanical technologies he had seen in high-technology firms. Conti returned and, under IDEO's aegis, founded a company called Edge Innovations that designs, builds, and operates realistic machines and creatures for films. Edge designed a life-size, 8,000-pound animatronic killer whale for the film *Free Willy* that audiences couldn't distinguish from Keiko, the real whale. (In fact, Keiko tried to mate with the mechanical killer whale.)

The best knowledge brokers are relentlessly curious. They're also fairly casual about where an idea comes from, as long as it works. Intense curiosity and a willingness to beg and borrow prompt people to reach out, early and often, to anyone who might have useful ideas.

As their openness to others' ideas suggests, good brokers are not arrogant. But they hardly lack confidence. An internal consultant told us that she has realized she needs to "swagger" while selling ideas she has seen elsewhere in the company: "If you act like you don't believe in the ideas, why should anybody else believe they're any good?" This balance between willingness to listen and hubris is reflected in an informal test applied by James Robbins, who has helped launch at least ten incubators in areas including computer software, e-commerce, and the environment. Robbins uses an "ego scale" as one way to screen staff for start-ups.

On a scale of one to ten, he looks for people who are at about a seven or eight. Tens act as if they knew everything and had nothing to learn; threes and fours—however bright they are—lack the confidence to be successful entrepreneurs.

The characteristics we've described—curiosity, a habit of reaching out for ideas and help, and a mixture of confidence and humility—help create a highly collaborative culture within knowledge-brokering firms or groups. The companies use financial rewards to further support collaborative behaviors. People in Idealab! companies not only get equity in their own start-ups, they get equity in Idealab! itself to encourage them to help other companies in the group. At IDEO, financial rewards are based in part on the reviews each person gets from colleagues.

Money is just part of the picture. The respect of peers is an important factor too. At several IDEO studios we visited, designers who focused on their own projects and didn't take time to help others were shunned and bad-mouthed. As one engineer told us, "At the first hint I don't know something, I ask, 'Does anyone know about this?' If you don't ask for help here, you're incompetent—you're useless to us." Conversely, designers who consistently contribute great ideas in brainstorming sessions not only gain respect from peers, they are invited to work on the most technically challenging and fun design projects.

Originally published in May–June 2000
Reprint R00304

Knowing a Winning Business Idea When You See One

W. CHAN KIM AND RENÉE MAUBORGNE

Executive Summary

IDENTIFYING WHICH BUSINESS IDEAS have real commercial potential is fraught with uncertainty, and even the most admired companies have stumbled. It's not as if they don't know what the challenges of innovation are. A new product has to offer customers exceptional utility at an attractive price, and the company must be able to deliver it at a tidy profit. But the uncertainties surrounding innovation are so great that even the most insightful managers have a hard time evaluating the commercial readiness of new business ideas.

In this article, W. Chan Kim and Renée Mauborgne introduce three tools that managers can use to help strip away some of that uncertainty. The first tool, "the buyer utility map," indicates how likely it is that customers will be attracted to a new business idea. The second, "the price corridor of the mass," identifies what price will unlock the greatest number of customers. And the third tool, "the business model guide," offers a framework for figuring out whether and how a company can profitably deliver the new idea at the targeted price.

Applying the tools, though, is not the end of the story. Many innovations have to overcome adoption hurdles—strong resistance from stakeholders inside and outside the company. Often overlooked in the planning process, adoption hurdles can make or break the commercial viability of even the most powerful new ideas. The authors conclude by discussing how managers can head off negative reactions from stakeholders.

In 1998, MOTOROLA rolled out a product that was supposed to redefine the world of mobile telephony. The Iridium, declared the company, would be the first mobile phone to provide uninterrupted wireless communication anywhere in the world, no matter what the terrain or country. It was a complete flop. In its rush to embrace a new technology, Motorola overlooked the product's many drawbacks: the phone was heavy, it needed a host of attachments, and it couldn't be used in a car or building—exactly where jet-setting global executives needed it most. At $3,000, people couldn't see any compelling reason to switch from their $150 cell phones.

As this tale illustrates, even the most admired companies can get innovation spectacularly wrong. Sometimes companies rush a new technology to market too soon or at the wrong price. At other times, they ignore the radical idea that another company uses to put them out of business. CNN's competitors, for example, first dismissed its offerings as "Chicken Noodle News."

It's not as if companies don't know what the challenges of innovation are. A new product has to offer customers exceptional utility at an attractive price, and the company must be able to deliver it at a tidy profit. But the uncertainties surrounding innovation are so great that even the most insightful managers have a hard time evaluating the commercial readiness and potential of new business ideas.

In this article, we offer a systematic approach to reducing the uncertainties of innovation. To understand what underpins the commercial success of a new idea, we've built up a database of more than 100 companies that have innovated successfully and repeatedly. We've also collected data on the companies whose products and services our innovators have displaced. (For more detail on our methodology, see "Our Research on Innovation" at the end of this article.) From that information, we created three analytic tools to help managers know a winning business idea when they see one—whatever the market space it occupies or creates. The first tool, "the buyer utility map," indicates the likelihood that customers will be attracted to the new idea. The second tool, "the price corridor of the mass," identifies what price will unlock the greatest number of customers. The third tool, "the business model guide," offers a framework for figuring out whether and how a company can profitably deliver the new idea at the targeted price.

Applying the tools, though, is not the end of the story. Many innovations have had to overcome adoption hurdles—strong resistance from stakeholders both inside and outside the company. While often overlooked in the planning process, adoption hurdles can make or break the commercial viability of even the most powerful innovative ideas. So we'll conclude by discussing how managers can head off those reactions. First, though, let's look at utility.

Creating Exceptional Utility

The managers at Motorola responsible for the Iridium fell into a very common trap: they reveled in the bells and whistles of their new technology. But successful innovators focus on the product's utility—that is, they try to identify where and how the new product or service will change the lives of its consumers. Such a difference in perspective is important because it means that how a product is developed becomes less a function of its technical possibilities and more a function of its utility to customers.

The buyer utility map helps to get managers thinking from the right perspective. It outlines all the levers companies can pull to deliver utility to customers as well as the different experiences customers can have of a product or service. This lets managers identify the full range of utility propositions that a product or service can offer. Let's look at the map's dimensions in detail. (See the exhibit "The Buyer Utility Map.")

THE SIX STAGES OF THE BUYER EXPERIENCE CYCLE

A customer's experience can usually be broken down into a cycle of six distinct stages, running more or less sequentially from purchase to disposal. Each stage encompasses a wide variety of specific experiences. Purchasing, for example, includes the experience of browsing Amazon.com as well as the experience of pushing a shopping cart through Wal-Mart's aisles. (The sidebar "Uncovering the Buyer Experience Cycle" provides a set of questions that managers can ask to gauge the quality of the buyer's experience at each stage.)

The Buyer Utility Map

By locating a new product on one of the 36 spaces shown here, managers can clearly see how the new idea creates a different utility proposition from existing products.

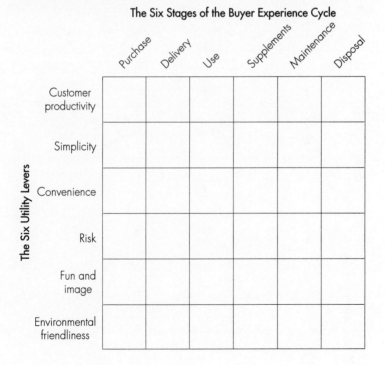

Uncovering the Buyer Experience Cycle

A customer's product experience passes through six basic stages. To help companies assess the quality of a buyer's total experience, we have identified the key questions for each stage. Individually, these questions may be obvious, but taken together, they uncover the full picture of the experience cycle.

The Buyer Experience Cycle

Purchase	Delivery	Use	Supplements	Maintenance	Disposal
• How long does it take to find the product you need? • Is the place of purchase attractive and accessible? • How secure is the transaction environment? • How rapidly can you make a purchase?	• How long does it take to get the product delivered? • How difficult is it to unpack and install the new product?	• Does the product require training or expert assistance? • Is the product easy to store when not in use? • How effective are the product's features and functions?	• Do you need other products and services to make this product work? • If so, how costly are they?	• Does the product require external maintenance? • How easy is it to maintain and upgrade the product?	• Does use of the product create waste items? • How easy is it to dispose of the product?

THE SIX UTILITY LEVERS

Cutting across the stages of the buyer's experience are
what we call the levers of utility—the ways in which
companies unlock utility for their customers. Most of the
levers are obvious. Simplicity, fun and image, and environmental friendliness need little explanation. Nor does
the idea that a product could reduce a customer's financial or physical risks. And a product or service offers convenience simply by being easy to obtain or use. The most
commonly used lever—but perhaps the least obvious—is
that of customer productivity. An innovation can
increase customers' productivity by helping them do
their thing faster, better, or in different ways. The financial information company Bloomberg, for example,
makes traders more efficient by offering on-line analytics
that quickly analyze and compare the raw information it
delivers.

By locating a new product on one of the 36 spaces of
the buyer utility map, managers can clearly see how the
new idea creates a different utility proposition from
existing products. In our experience, managers all too
often focus on delivering more of the same utility at the
same stage of the buyer's experience. That approach may
be reasonable in emerging industries, where there's
plenty of room for improving a company's current utility
proposition. But in many existing industries, this
approach is unlikely to produce market-shaping innovations. Let's look instead at how successful innovators
have staked out new spaces on the map.

Using a new utility lever at the same stage. Many
successful innovations create new expectations for a
familiar experience. Starbucks, which has revolutionized

the American office-worker's coffee break, is a case in point. Traditionally, people bought coffee in delis or fast-food chains—businesses that competed by offering customers fast and cheap coffee. In terms of the map, those companies focused on delivering customer productivity in the purchasing experience. Starbucks, however, moved into a new space entirely. By establishing chic coffee bars that offer an exotic mix of brews, the company injected fun and cachet into the coffee-purchasing experience. As a result, middle class America has become coffee literate, and coffee bars have become American fixtures.

Using the same utility lever in a new stage. Companies can also innovate by extending a familiar utility to different parts of the customer's product or service experience. That's how Michael Dell changed the computer business. Computer manufacturers used to compete by offering faster computers with more features and software. In terms of the map, they offered customers more productivity in the use of the machines. Dell extended the same utility to the delivery experience. By bypassing dealers, Dell delivers PCs tailored to customers' needs faster than any other computer manufacturer.

Using a new utility lever in a new stage. In some industries, the most rewarding innovations do something completely new. A good example of this kind of innovation is the Alto, a disposable fluorescent bulb manufactured by European electronics giant Philips. Most lightbulb manufacturers competed to offer customers more productivity in use; they did not pay much attention to the fact that the bulbs had to be carted off to special dumping sites because of their harmful mercury content. By creating a fluorescent bulb that could be disposed of in an environmentally friendly manner, Philips moved into and dominated a utility space largely ignored by its competitors. In the first year alone, the Alto poached more than 25% of traditional fluorescent lamp sales in the United States while enjoying superior margins.

Beyond highlighting the differences between ideas that are genuine innovations and those that are essentially revisions of existing offerings, the buyer utility map reminds executives just how many unexplored innovation possibilities there are. Even the most productive innovators end up occupying only a small number of the 36 utility spaces. (For an example of how one innovative company's business ideas look on the map, see "How Schwab Created Exceptional Utility" at the end of this article.) Think for a moment of your own industry. How many spaces does your company occupy?

Setting a Strategic Price

Offering exceptional utility alone doesn't make an innovation successful. You also have to set the right price. In the old days, that wasn't such an immediate issue. Companies could test the waters by targeting novelty-seeking, price-insensitive customers at the launch and then drop prices over time to attract mainstream buyers. But in the new economy, managers have to know from the start what price will quickly create a large pool of customers.

There are two reasons why it has become critical to reach a high volume very quickly. First, companies are discovering that in more and more businesses, volume generates higher returns than it used to. That's because these days, as the nature of goods becomes more knowledge intensive, companies bear much more of their costs in product development than in manufacturing. So once the development costs have been covered, sales fall straight to the bottom line. A second reason is that some companies have no choice but to seize the mass market early. The value to a customer of a product or

Market-shaping innovations win by creating new customer pools, not by increasing the share of an existing customer pool.

service such as the on-line auctions managed by eBay, for example, is closely tied to the total number of people using it. Customers who think hardly anyone else is using a product or service will not buy it either. As a result of this phenomenon, called network externalities, many products and services are an all-or-nothing proposition: either you sell millions at once or you sell nothing at all.

The price you choose for a product must not only attract customers in large numbers but also help you to retain them. We call this strategic pricing. Many innovations are extremely vulnerable to imitation. The Starbucks and Home Depot concepts, for example, are not ideas that can be protected by patents. For customers to remain loyal, they must be convinced that they will not find better value with an imitator. A company's reputation has to be earned on day one, because brand building these days relies heavily on word-of-mouth recommendations spreading rapidly through our networked society. Companies, therefore, must start with an offer that customers just can't refuse. Our next tool, the price corridor of the mass, will help managers find the right price for that irresistible offer—which, by the way, isn't necessarily the lowest price. The tool involves two distinct but interrelated steps. (See the exhibit "The Price Corridor of the Mass.")

STEP 1: IDENTIFYING THE PRICE CORRIDOR OF THE MASS

In setting a price, all companies look first at the products and services that most closely resemble their idea in

---

The Price Corridor of the Mass

To find the right price for your new product, you must first identify the price corridor of the mass—that is, the price bandwidth that captures the largest group of customers. Then, depending on how much legal and resource protection you have, determine how high a price you can set without inviting in competitors with imitation products.

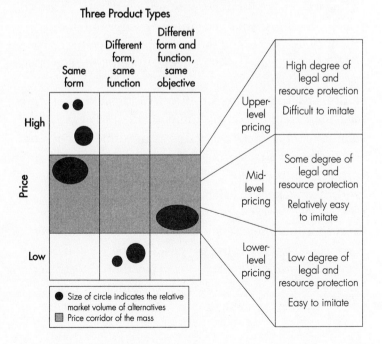

terms of form—that is, other products within their
industries. That's still a necessary exercise, of course, but
market-shaping innovations win by creating new customer pools, not by just increasing the share of an existing customer pool. So the main challenge in determining
a strategic price is understanding the price sensitivities
of people who will be comparing the new product with a
host of very different-looking products and services
offered by companies outside the group of traditional
competitors. For some companies, identifying a product's potential customers is straightforward. In pricing
short-haul trips, for example, Southwest Airlines only
had to look beyond other airlines' customers to people
using buses, trains, and cars. Other companies, however,
may not find the exercise so easy. A good way to get
executives to look outside their industry's boundaries is
to have them list products and services that fall into two
categories: those that take different forms but perform
the same function, and those that take different forms
and functions but share the same over-arching objective.

Different form, same function. Many successful innovations attract customers from other industries who use
a product or service that performs the same function or
core utility as the new one but takes a very different
physical form. Most people who use Intuit's financial
software package Quicken, for example, buy it not
because it is a software product but because it helps
them sort out their personal finances. The alternatives to
using Quicken are to use pencil and paper—a tedious
and error-prone approach—or to pay for the costly services of a CPA. The CPA, the pencil, and the software
product offer the same functionality or core utility—

namely, they help people organize and understand their financial affairs.

Different form and function, same objective. Some innovations have lured customers from even further away. The European cinema chain Kinepolis, for example, has diverted customers from a wide range of evening activities. In Brussels, it expanded the number of moviegoers by more than 40% with its first Megaplex. This growth came in part through drawing people away from other activities that differed in both form and function. For example, bars and restaurants have few physical features in common with a cinema. What's more, restaurants and bars serve a distinct function. They provide conversational and gastronomical pleasure—a very different experience from the visual entertainment that cinema offers. Yet despite these differences in form and function, people go to a bar or restaurant for the same broad reason they go to the movies—to enjoy a night out.

The exercise of listing the groups of alternative products and services will allow managers to see the full range of customers they can poach from other industries as well as from direct competitors. Managers should then graphically plot the price and volume of these alternatives, as shown in the exhibit. This provides a fairly straightforward way to identify where the largest groups of potential customers are and what prices they are prepared to pay for the products and services they currently use. The price bandwidth that captures the largest groups of customers is what we call the price corridor of the mass. In some cases, the range is very wide. For Southwest Airlines, for example, the largest groups of potential customers were paying on average $400 to buy an economy class short-haul ticket (short-haul being a 400-mile journey) or about $60 for the cost of going the same distance by car.

STEP 2: SPECIFYING A LEVEL WITHIN THE PRICE CORRIDOR

The second part of the tool helps managers determine how high a price they can afford to set within the corridor without inviting in competitors with imitation products. That assessment depends on the degree to which the product or service is protected legally through patents or copyrights and on the company's ownership of some exclusive asset, such as an expensive production plant or an established brand name. Obviously, companies that have no such protection must set a relatively low price. Going back to the Southwest Airlines example, because its service wasn't patentable and required no exclusive assets, its ticket prices fell in the lower boundary of the corridor—namely, against the price of car travel. But some products are protected enough to merit a high price. Dyson Vacuum Cleaners, for example, has been able to charge a high unit price for its bagless cleaners since the product's launch in 1995, thanks to both strong patents and an outstanding service capability. Few companies, however, are as insulated from competitors as Dyson is. Companies with uncertain patent and asset protection should consider pricing somewhere in the middle of the corridor.

Building a Profitable Business Model

Utility and price are only part of the story. At the end of the day, every company—dot-coms included—has to turn a profit. Successful innovators have lean and profitable business models from the outset. And a good business model is itself a powerful defense against imitation. The fact that CNN, for example, could produce 24 hours of news at one-fifth the hourly cost of network news fended off imitators for about 15 years.

There's no magic formula for finding that kind of business model, but we have developed a systematic way of thinking through the issues, which will help managers avoid some pitfalls. Our third tool, the business model guide, is a series of questions designed to open up the way managers think about production and distribution methods, their company's capabilities, and a pricing structure for the product. (See the exhibit "The Business Model Guide.")

WHAT IS THE COST TARGET?

In our experience, companies have a hard time keeping down the costs of new products, and to compensate, they usually set prices far higher than would be strategically wise. Successful innovators, however, never let costs dictate price. By basing their cost targets on the market-driven strategic price and refusing to allow for overruns, they force their organizations to question virtually every assumption about materials, design, and manufacturing—often with surprising results. The Swiss watch company Swatch is a case in point. At the start, founder Nicholas Hayek set a $40 price target for watches and mandated that the company create a product that could hit a target profit margin at that price. Given the high cost of Swiss labor, Swatch could achieve Hayek's goal only by making radical changes to the product and production methods. Instead of using the more traditional

The Business Model Guide

The questions "What is the cost target?" and "Who can we partner with?" are closely related. That's because a company's cost target will influence how it obtains the capabilities it needs, and the capabilities it needs will affect its ability to change its cost structure. Once costs and capabilities are optimized toward the cost target, which is driven by the strategic price, the company should challenge the industry's standard pricing model to reach more customers and increase profitability.

What is the cost target?

- Is your cost target set by the strategic price?

- Can the product's raw materials be replaced by unconventional, less expensive ones?

- Did you significantly eliminate, reduce, and outsource high-cost, low-value-added activities in your value chain?

- Can you reduce costs by digitizing assets or activities?

Who can we partner with?

- What capabilities do you need to achieve the value proposition, and which ones do you lack?

- Which companies have those missing capabilities?

- Based on cost, quality, and speed, should you acquire those companies or partner with them?

Which price model should we use?

- Is your industry's pricing model a barrier to your business idea's success?

- What pricing model—direct selling, leasing, time-share, slice-share, or equity payment—would create a greater profit pool?

metal or leather, for example, Swatch used plastic. Swatch's engineers also drastically simplified the design of the watch's inner workings, reducing the number of parts from 150 to 51. Finally, the engineers developed new and cheaper assembly techniques—for instance, the watchcases were sealed by ultrasonic welding instead of screws. Taken together, the design and manufacturing changes enabled Swatch to reduce direct labor costs from 30% to less than 10% of total costs. In the end, the total manufacturing costs of the Swatch were almost 30% less than those of competing products from Hong Kong. These cost innovations let the Swiss company profitably compete in the mass market for watches—a market previously dominated by Asian manufacturers with a cheaper labor pool.

WHO CAN WE PARTNER WITH?

In bringing a product to market, many innovators mistakenly try to carry out all the production and distribution activities themselves. Often, that's because they see the product as a platform for developing new capabilities. But unless the product is extremely well protected against imitation, this approach can be a recipe for disaster; time works against the innovator in favor of the imitator.

Consider EMI, which developed the CAT scanner, a medical device that earned creator Godfrey Houndsfield the Nobel Prize. Despite having no experience in the medical industry and no presence to speak of in the United States, the largest and most demanding market for advanced medical equipment, EMI tried to build its own distribution capability there. Unfortunately, the

CAT scanner, although a medical breakthrough, was highly susceptible to imitation because its basic technologies were well established. Within three years, a host of CAT scanners manufactured by electronic giants like GE and Siemens were jostling for U.S. market share. The same year Houndsfield won his Nobel Prize, EMI had to sell its scanner unit to Thorn Electric.

Savvy innovators are increasingly eschewing organic growth and instead filling the gaps in their capabilities by partnering and acquiring. That allows them to move quickly and expertly. SAP, which rapidly grew to become the world leader in enterprise resource planning (ERP) software, had serious gaps both in its technology and in its distribution capabilities at its founding in 1972. Rather than cultivate capabilities internally, it acquired them. For example, SAP partnered with Oracle to gain access to the central database software that sits at the heart of SAP's core products R/2 and R/3. SAP also found partners to help it install and implement the product, namely consulting firms such as Arthur Andersen and Cap Gemini, which could leverage their strong networks among SAP's target customers. And it acquired companies such German-based iXOS Software to gain access to UNIX expertise rapidly. SAP's willingness to look outside the company to fill missing capabilities is one reason it has remained a world leader in business application software. And its success in the future will depend on its ability to keep reaching out in this way.

WHICH PRICE MODEL SHOULD WE USE?

Sometimes it seems that no amount of redesign or partnering will make it possible for a company to provide a product or service at the required strategic price. In such cases, it is very likely that managers have fallen into the trap of assuming too much about the way a product or service should be priced. When film videotapes first came out, for example, they were priced at around $80. Few people were willing to pay that amount because no one expected to watch the video more than two or three times.

Successful innovators never assume that there's only one way to price a product. Blockbuster Video, for example, got around the cost-price problem in its industry by changing the pricing model from selling to renting. At only a few dollars a rental, the home video market exploded; Blockbuster made more money by repeatedly renting the same $80 videos than it could have by selling them outright.

In addition to Blockbuster's rental model, innovators have used several other pricing models to bring expensive products within the reach of the mass market. One is the time-share. The New Jersey company Executive Jet follows this model to make jets accessible to a wide range of corporate customers, who buy the right to use a jet for a certain amount of time rather than buying the jet itself. Another model is the slice-share; mutual fund managers, for instance, bring high-quality portfolio services—traditionally provided by private banks to the rich—to the small investor by selling a sliver of the portfolio rather than its whole. Some companies are abandoning the concept of price altogether. Instead, they give products to customers in return for an equity interest in the customer's business. Hewlett-Packard, for example, trades high-powered servers to Silicon Valley start-ups for a share of their revenues. The customers get immediate access to a key capability, and HP stands to earn a lot more than the price of the machine. The aim is not to compromise on the strategic price but to hit the target through a new price model.

Overcoming Adoption Hurdles

Even an outstanding value proposition and an unbeatable business model may not be enough to guarantee a product's success. Almost by definition, innovations threaten the status quo, and for that reason often provoke fear and resistance among a company's three main stakeholders—its employees, its business partners, and the general public. Would-be innovators ignore those reactions at their peril. As with most fears, the way to overcome a fear of innovation is by educating the fearful.

EMPLOYEES

Failure to adequately address the concerns of employees about the impact an innovation may have on their livelihoods can be expensive. When Merrill Lynch's management, for example, announced plans to create an on-line brokerage service, its stock price fell by 14% as reports emerged of resistance and infighting within the company's large retail brokerage division. Smart innovators, therefore, make a concerted effort to communicate to employees that the company is aware of the threats an innovation poses before going public with it. They work with employees to find ways of defusing the threats so that everyone in the company wins, despite shifts in people's roles, responsibilities, and rewards. In contrast to Merrill Lynch, Morgan Stanley Dean Witter engaged employees in an open internal discussion of the company's strategy for meeting the challenge of the Internet. Morgan's efforts paid off handsomely. Because the market realized that Morgan's employees understood the need for an e-venture, the company's shares rose by 13% when it eventually announced the venture.

BUSINESS PARTNERS

Potentially even more damaging than employee disaffection is the resistance of partners who fear that their revenue streams or market positions are threatened by a new idea. That was the problem faced by SAP when it was developing its product AcceleratedSAP (ASAP)—a faster-to-implement version of R/3. ASAP brought ERP within the reach of midsized and small companies for the first time. The problem was that the development of best-practice templates for ASAP required the active cooperation of large consulting firms that were deriving substantial income from implementations of SAP's other products. SAP resolved the dilemma by openly discussing the issues with its partners. Its executives convinced the consulting firms that they stood to gain more business by cooperating. Although ASAP would reduce implementation time for small and midsized companies, consultants would gain access to a new ERP client base that would more than compensate for some lost revenues from larger companies. It would also offer consultants a way to respond to customers' increasingly vocal concerns that ERP software took too long to implement.

THE GENERAL PUBLIC

Opposition to an innovation can also spread to the general public—especially if the innovation is the result of a technological breakthrough that threatens established social or political norms. The effects can be devastating.

Consider Monsanto, which makes genetically modified foods. It has become a figure of questionable intentions among European consumers—who should be customers—thanks to the efforts of environmental groups such as Greenpeace, Friends of the Earth, and the Soil Association. The attacks of these groups have struck many chords in Europe, which has a history of environmental concern and powerful agricultural lobbies.

Monsanto's mistake was to let other people take charge of the debate. It should have educated both the environmental groups and the public on the benefits of genetically modified food and its potential to eliminate world famine and disease. Once the products came out, Monsanto should have given consumers a choice between organic and genetically modified foods by labeling which products had genetically modified seeds as their base. Had Monsanto taken these steps, instead of being vilified, it might have ended up as the "Intel Inside" of food for the future—the provider of the essential technology.

In educating these three groups of stakeholders, the key challenge is to engage in an open discussion about why the innovation is necessary, explain its merits, and set clear expectations of the innovation's ramifications and how the company will address them. Stakeholders need to know that their voices have been heard and that there will be no surprises. Companies that take the trouble to have such a dialogue with stakeholders will find that it amply repays the time and effort involved. (For a fuller discussion of how companies can engage stakeholders—employees in particular—see our article "Fair Process: Managing in the Knowledge Economy" in the July–August 1997 issue of HBR.)

TROUBLES LIKE MOTOROLA'S IRIDIUM and Monsanto's genetically modified foods give innovation a bad name. But when innovations do succeed they can create compelling new businesses and even whole new industries. AOL, for instance, did more than create an Internet portal; it virtually created the industry of Internet service providers. With all the uncertainties around innovation, it is perhaps unsurprising that many managers regard it as something of a lottery: you have to pay for a lot of mistakes to hit the jackpot. There's some truth in that view, of course. There will always be an element of chance— even magic—about innovation. No one has a crystal ball.

But we believe that the framework presented here strips much of the mystery away and brings innovation firmly into the realm of plannable business. If a new idea passes its evaluation by the tools introduced here, and if it is fairly communicated to stakeholders, managers can be confident that they have found a winner. But our framework does more than just evaluate individual new ideas. By revealing what makes a new idea a commercial success, it enables companies to develop a coherent strategy for becoming successful at business innovation. To put it another way, the tools help companies not only to recognize a winner when they see one but also to know where to start looking in the first place.

How Schwab Created Exceptional Utility

ONE OF THE MOST INNOVATIVE COMPANIES in our database is the discount broker Charles Schwab. Schwab's first innovation was to make customers feel safe about trading over the phone and later on-line. At a time when most discount brokers were competing on price, Schwab recognized that customers were actually more concerned about the safe execution of their trades. By providing instantaneous computer confirmation, Schwab eliminated that perceived risk.

Schwab then went on to make purchasing more convenient. Most discount brokers were only open during normal office hours—which was not when customers were free. Customers' problems were compounded by the fact that they had to transfer the funds for their stock trades from their banks, which had even more restrictive hours and much slower response times than brokers.

The Six Stages of the Buyer Experience Cycle

	Purchase	Delivery	Use	Supplements	Maintenance	Disposal
Customer productivity						
Simplicity					OneSource	
Convenience	24/7 service Schwab One cash management account					
Risk	Secure transactions Instantaneous confirmations					
Fun and image						
Environmental friendliness						

The Six Utility Levers

Schwab offered 24-hour, seven-day-a-week service and a Schwab One cash management account with checking privileges and Visa Card, allowing customers to sidestep those inconveniences.

Schwab's next innovation came in the simplicity and maintenance space. It saw how complex it was for customers to track their mutual fund investments. Customers would typically receive statements of their mutual fund accounts from each fund company they dealt with. They would then be burdened with putting all the pieces together to see the bigger picture of their financial performance. Schwab launched OneSource, a service that gives customers a monthly consolidated statement of all mutual fund investments purchased through Schwab. Schwab has gone on to explore new utility spaces and has kept ahead of the pack. Whether or not Schwab will continue to lead rests on its ability to keep staking out new utility spaces before its competitors do.

Our Research on Innovation

MORE THAN A DECADE AGO, we researched the roots of profitable growth and found that innovation is the key driver—a finding consistent with the New Growth Theory of economics spearheaded by Paul Romer at Stanford University. Since then, our research has focused on how companies actually make innovations happen. We began by building up a comprehensive database that tracks over 30 successful, innovative companies in as many different industries.

Over time, as the Internet took off and dot-com companies began proliferating, our database expanded to

include more than 100 companies—some that have succeeded at innovation and some that have failed. We
have interviewed hundreds of managers at these companies and systematically compared their successes and
failures.

In our previous HBR articles, we have drawn on our
research to describe how the innovations of successful
companies have reshaped their industries or even created new ones (See "Value Innovation: The Strategic
Logic of High Growth," January–February 1997, and
Chapter 1, "Creating New Market Space.") We have
also described how companies can create a working
environment to generate, share, and build new ideas
and knowledge. In this article, we move from the industries and companies to the innovations themselves. And
we introduce a set of analytic tools that managers can
use to assess the commercial potential of any innovative
idea.

Originally published in September–October 2000
Reprint R00510

Meeting the Challenge of Disruptive Change

CLAYTON M. CHRISTENSEN AND
MICHAEL OVERDORF

Executive Summary

WHY DIDN'T A SINGLE minicomputer company succeed in the personal computer business? Why did only one department store—Dayton Hudson—become a leader in discount retailing? Why can't large companies capitalize on the opportunities brought about by major, disruptive changes in their markets?

It's because organizations, independent of the people in them, have capabilities. And those capabilities also define disabilities. As a company grows, what it can and cannot do becomes more sharply defined in certain predictable ways. The authors have analyzed those patterns to create a framework managers can use to assess the abilities and disabilities of their organization as a whole.

When a company is young, its resources—its people, equipment, technologies, cash, brands, suppliers, and the like—define what it can and cannot do. As it becomes more mature, its abilities stem more from its processes—product development, manufacturing, budgeting, for example. In the largest companies, values—particularly those that determine what are its acceptable gross margins and how big and opportunity has to be before it becomes interesting—define what the company can and cannot do. Because resources are more adaptable to change than processes or values, smaller companies tend to respond to major market shifts better than larger ones.

The authors suggest ways large companies can capitalize on opportunities that normally would not fit in with their processes or values; it all starts with understanding what the organizations are capable of.

THESE ARE SCARY TIMES for managers in big companies. Even before the Internet and globalization, their track record for dealing with major, disruptive change was not good. Out of hundreds of department sores, for example, only one—Dayton Hudson—became a leader in discount retailing. Not one of the minicomputer companies succeeded in the personal computer business. Medical and business schools are struggling—and failing—to change their curricula fast enough to train the types of doctors and managers their markets need. The list could go on.

It's not that managers in big companies can't see disruptive changes coming. Usually they can. Nor do they lack resources to confront them. Most big companies have talented managers and specialists, strong product portfolios, first-rate technological know-how, and deep pockets. What managers lack is a habit of thinking about their organization's capabilities as carefully as they think about individual people's capabilities.

One of the hallmarks of a great manager is the ability to identify the right person for the right job and to train employees to succeed at the jobs they're given. But unfortunately, most managers assume that if each person working on a project is well matched to the job, then the organization in which they work will be, too. Often that is not the case. One could put two sets of identically capable people to work in different organizations, and what they accomplished would be significantly different. That's because organizations themselves—independent of the people and other resources in them—have capabilities. To succeed consistently, good managers need to be skilled not just in assessing people but also in assessing the abilities and disabilities of their organization as a whole.

This article offers managers a framework to help them understand what their organizations are capable of accomplishing. It will show them how their company's disabilities become more sharply defined even as its core capabilities grow. It will give them a way to recognize different kinds of change and make appropriate organizational responses to the opportunities that arise from each. And it will offer some bottom-line advice that runs counter to much that's assumed in our can-do business culture: if an organization faces major change—a disruptive innovation, perhaps—the worst possible approach may be to make drastic adjustments to the existing organization. In trying to transform an enterprise, managers can destroy the very capabilities that sustain it.

Before rushing into the breach, managers must understand precisely what types of change the existing organization is capable and incapable of handling. To help them do that, we'll first take a systematic look at how to recognize a company's core capabilities on an organizational level and then examine how those capabilities migrate as companies grow and mature.

Where Capabilities Reside

Our research suggests that three factors affect what an organization can and cannot do: its resources, its processes, and its values. When thinking about what sorts of innovations their organization will be able to embrace, managers need to assess how each of these factors might affect their organization's capacity to change.

RESOURCES

When they ask the question, "What can this company do?" the place most managers look for the answer is in its resources—both the tangible ones like people, equipment, technologies, and cash, and the less tangible ones like product designs, information, brands, and relationships with suppliers, distributors, and customers. Without doubt, access to abundant, high-quality resources increases an organization's chances of coping with change. But resource analysis doesn't come close to telling the whole story.

PROCESSES

The second factor that affects what a company can and cannot do is its processes. By processes, we mean the patterns of interaction, coordination, communication, and decision making employees use to transform resources into products and services of greater worth. Such examples as the processes that govern product development, manufacturing, and budgeting come immediately to mind. Some processes are formal, in the sense that they are explicitly defined and documented. Others are informal: they are routines or ways of working that evolve over time. The former tend to be more visible, the latter less visible.

One of the dilemmas of management is that processes, by their very nature, are set up so that employees perform tasks in a consistent way, time after time. They are *meant* not to change or, if they must change, to change through tightly controlled procedures. When people use a process to do the task it was designed for, it is likely to perform efficiently. But when the same process is used to tackle a very different task, it is likely to perform sluggishly. Companies focused on developing and winning FDA approval for new drug compounds, for example, often prove inept at developing and winning approval for medical devices because the second task entails very different ways of working. In fact, a process that creates the capability to execute one task concurrently defines disabilities in executing other tasks.[1]

The most important capabilities and concurrent disabilities aren't necessarily embodied in the most visible processes, like logistics, development, manufacturing, or customer service. In fact, they are more likely to be in the less visible, background processes that support decisions about where to invest resources—those that define how market research is habitually done, how such analysis is translated into financial projections, how plans and budgets are negotiated internally, and so on. It is in those processes that many organizations' most serious disabilities in coping with change reside.

VALUES

The third factor that affects what an organization can and cannot do is its values. Sometimes the phrase "corporate values" carries an ethical connotation: one thinks of the principles that ensure patient well-being for Johnson & Johnson or that guide decisions about employee safety at Alcoa. But within our framework, "values" has a broader meaning. We define an organization's values as the standards by which employees set priorities that enable them to judge whether an order is attractive or unattractive, whether a customer is more important or less important, whether an idea for a new product is attractive or marginal, and so on. Prioritization decisions are made by employees at every level. Among salespeople, they consist of on-the-spot, day-to-day decisions about which products to push with customers and which to de-emphasize. At the executive tiers, they often take the form of decisions to invest, or not, in new products, services, and processes.

The larger and more complex a company becomes, the more important it is for senior managers to train employees throughout the organization to make independent decisions about priorities that are consistent with the strategic direction and the business model of the company. A key metric of good management, in fact, is whether such clear, consistent values have permeated the organization.

But consistent, broadly understood values also define what an organization cannot do. A company's values reflect its cost structure or its business model because those define the rules its employees must follow for the company to prosper. If, for example, a company's overhead costs require it to achieve gross profit margins of 40%, then a value or decision rule will have evolved that encourages middle managers to kill ideas that promise gross margins below 40%. Such an organization would be incapable of commercializing projects targeting low-margin markets—such as those in e-commerce—even though another organization's values, driven by a very different cost structure, might facilitate the success of the same project.

Different companies, of course, embody different values. But we want to focus on two sets of values in particular that tend to evolve in most companies in very predictable ways.The inexorable evolution of these two values is what makes companies progressively less capable of addressing disruptive change successfully.

As in the previous example, the first value dictates the way the company judges acceptable gross margins. As companies add features and functions to their products and services, trying to capture more attractive customers in premium tiers of their markets, they often add overhead cost. As a result, gross margins that were once attractive become unattractive. For instance, Toyota entered the North American market with the Corona model, which targeted the lower end of the market. As that segment

One of the bittersweet results of success is that as companies become large, they lose sight of small, emerging markets.

became crowded with look-alike models from Honda, Mazda, and Nissan, competition drove down profit margins. To improve its margins, Toyota then developed more sophisticated cars targeted at higher tiers. The process of developing cars like the Camry and the Lexus added costs to Toyota's operation. It subsequently decided to exit the lower end of the market; the margins had become unacceptable because the company's cost structure, and consequently its values, had changed.

In a departure from that pattern, Toyota recently introduced the Echo model, hoping to rejoin the entry-level tier with a $10,000 car. It is one thing for Toyota's senior management to decide to launch this new model. It's another for the many people in the Toyota system—including its dealers—to agree that selling more cars at lower margins is a better way to boost profits and equity values than selling more Camrys, Avalons, and Lexuses. Only time will tell whether Toyota can manage this down-market move. To be successful with the Echo, Toyota's management will have to swim against a very strong current—the current of its own corporate values.

The second value relates to how big a business opportunity has to be before it can be interesting. Because a company's stock price represents the discounted present value of its projected earnings stream, most managers feel compelled not just to maintain growth but to maintain a constant rate of growth. For a $40 million company to grow 25%, for instance, it needs to find $10 million in new business the next year. But a $40 billion company needs to find $10 billion in new business the next year to grow at that same rate. It follows that an opportunity that excites a small company isn't big enough to be interesting to a large company. One of the bittersweet results of success, in fact, is that as companies become large, they lose the ability to enter small, emerging markets. This disability is not caused by a change in the resources within the companies—their resources typically are vast. Rather, it's caused by an evolution in values.

The problem is magnified when companies suddenly become much bigger through mergers or acquisitions. Executives and Wall Street financiers who engineer megamergers between already-huge pharmaceutical companies, for example, need to take this effect into account. Although their merged research organizations might have more resources to throw at new product development, their commercial organizations will probably have lost their appetites for all but the biggest blockbuster drugs. This constitutes a very real disability in managing innovation. The same problem crops up in high-tech industries as well. In many ways, Hewlett-Packard's recent decision to split itself into two companies is rooted in its recognition of this problem.

The Migration of Capabilities

In the start-up stages of an organization, much of what gets done is attributable to resources—people, in particular. The addition or departure of a few key people can profoundly influence its success. Over time, however, the locus of the organization's capabilities shifts toward its processes and values. As people address recurrent tasks, processes become defined. And as the business model takes shape and it becomes clear which types of business need to be accorded highest priority, values coalesce. In fact, one reason that many soaring young companies flame out after an IPO based on a single hot product is that their initial success is grounded in resources—often the founding engineers—and they fail to develop processes that can create a sequence of hot products.

Avid Technology, a producer of digital-editing systems for television, is an apt case in point. Avid's well-received technology removed tedium from the video-editing process. On the back of its star product, Avid's stock rose from $16 a share at its 1993 IPO to $49 in mid-1995. However, the strains of being a one-trick pony soon emerged as Avid faced a saturated market, rising inventories and receivables, increased competition, and shareholder lawsuits. Customers loved the product, but Avid's lack of effective processes for consistently developing new products and for controlling quality, delivery, and service ultimately tripped the company and sent its stock back down.

By contrast, at highly successful firms such as McKinsey & Company, the processes and values have become so powerful that it almost doesn't matter which people get assigned to which project teams. Hundreds of MBAs join the firm every year, and almost as many leave. But the company is able to crank out high-quality work year after year because its core capabilities are rooted in its processes and values rather than in its resources.

When a company's processes and values are being formed in its early and middle years, the founder typically has a profound impact. The founder usually has strong opinions about how employees should do their work and what the organization's priorities need to be. If the founder's judgments are flawed, of course, the company will likely fail. But if they're sound, employees will experience for themselves the validity of the founder's problem-solving and decision-making methods. Thus processes become defined. Likewise, if the company becomes financially successful by allocating resources according to criteria that reflect the founder's priorities, the company's values coalesce around those criteria.

As successful companies mature, employees gradually come to assume that the processes and priorities they've used so successfully so often are the right way to do their work. Once that happens and employees begin to follow processes and decide priorities by assumption rather than by conscious choice, those processes and values come to constitute the organization's culture.[2] As companies grow from a few employees to hundreds and thousands of them, the challenge of getting all employees to agree on what needs to be done and how can be daunting for even the best managers. Culture is a powerful management tool in those situations. It enables employees to act autonomously but causes them to act consistently.

Hence, the factors that define an organization's capabilities and disabilities evolve over time—they start in resources; then move to visible, articulated processes and values; and migrate finally to culture. As long as the organization continues to face the same sorts of problems that its processes and values were designed to address, managing the organization can be straightforward. But because those factors also define what an organization cannot do, they constitute disabilities when the problems facing the company change fundamentally. When the organization's capabilities reside primarily in its people, changing capabilities to address the new problems is relatively simple. But when the capabilities have come to reside in processes and values, and especially when they have become embedded in culture, change can be extraordinarily difficult. (See "Digital's Dilemma" at the end of this article.)

Sustaining Versus Disruptive Innovation

Successful companies, no matter what the source of their capabilities, are pretty good at responding to evolutionary changes in their markets—what in *The Innovator's Dilemma* (Harvard Business School, 1997), Clayton Christensen referred to as *sustaining innovation.* Where they run into trouble is in handling or initiating revolutionary changes in their markets, or dealing with *disruptive innovation.*

Sustaining technologies are innovations that make a product or service perform better in ways that customers in the mainstream market already value. Compaq's early adoption of Intel's 32-bit 386 microprocessor instead of the 16-bit 286 chip was a sustaining innovation. So was Merrill Lynch's introduction of its Cash Management Account, which allowed customers to write checks against their equity accounts. Those were breakthrough innovations that sustained the best customers of these companies by providing something better than had previously been available.

Disruptive innovations create an entirely new market through the introduction of a new kind of product or service, one that's actually worse, initially, as judged by the performance metrics that mainstream customers value. Charles Schwab's initial entry as a barebones discount broker was a disruptive innovation relative to the offerings of full-service brokers like Merrill

Lynch. Merrill Lynch's best customers wanted more than Schwab-like services. Early personal computers were a disruptive innovation relative to mainframes and minicomputers. PCs were not powerful enough to run the computing applications that existed at the time they were introduced. These innovations were disruptive in that they didn't address the next-generation needs of leading customers in existing markets. They had other attributes, of course, that enabled new market applications to emerge—and the disruptive innovations improved so rapidly that they ultimately could address the needs of customers in the mainstream of the market as well.

Sustaining innovations are nearly always developed and introduced by established industry leaders. But those same companies never introduce—or cope well with—disruptive innovations. Why? Our resources-processes-values framework holds the answer. Industry leaders are organized to develop and introduce sustaining technologies. Month after month, year after year, they launch new and improved products to gain an edge over the competition. They do so by developing processes for evaluating the technological potential of sustaining innovations and for assessing their customers' needs for alternatives. Investment in sustaining technology also fits in with the values of leading companies in that they promise higher margins from better products sold to leading-edge customers.

Disruptive innovations occur so intermittently that no company has a routine process for handling them. Furthermore, because disruptive products nearly always promise lower profit margins per unit sold and are not attractive to the company's best customers, they're inconsistent with the established company's values. Merrill Lynch had the resources—the people, money, and technology—required to succeed at the sustaining innovations (Cash Management Account) and the disruptive innovations (bare-bones discount brokering) that it has confronted in recent history. But its processes and values supported only the sustaining innovation: they became disabilities when the company needed to understand and confront the discount and on-line brokerage businesses.

The reason, therefore, that large companies often surrender emerging growth markets is that smaller, disruptive companies are actually more capable of pursuing them. Start-ups lack resources, but that doesn't matter. Their values can embrace small markets, and their cost structures can accommodate low margins. Their market research and resource allocation processes allow managers to proceed intuitively; every decision need not be backed by careful research and analysis. All these advantages add up to the ability to embrace and even initiate disruptive change. But how can a large company develop those capabilities?

Creating Capabilities to Cope with Change

Despite beliefs spawned by popular change-management and reengineering programs, processes are not nearly as flexible or adaptable as resources are—and values are even less so. So whether addressing sustaining or disruptive innovations, when an organization needs new processes and values—because it needs new capabilities—managers must create a new organizational space where those capabilities can be developed. There are three possible ways to do that. Managers can

- create new organizational structures within corporate boundaries in which new processes can be developed,

- spin out an independent organization from the existing organization and develop within it the new processes and values required to solve the new problem,

- acquire a different organization whose processes and values closely match the requirements of the new task.

CREATING NEW CAPABILITIES INTERNALLY

When a company's capabilities reside in its processes, and when new challenges require new processes—that is, when they require different people or groups in a company to interact differently and at a different pace than they habitually have done—managers need to pull the relevant people out of the existing organization and draw a new boundary around a new group. Often, organizational boundaries were first drawn to facilitate the operation of existing processes, and they impede the creation of new processes. New team boundaries facilitate new patterns of working together that ultimately can coalesce as new processes. In *Revolutionizing Product Development* (The Free Press, 1992), Steven Wheelwright and Kim Clark referred to these structures as "heavyweight teams."

These teams are entirely dedicated to the new challenge, team members are physically located together, and each member is charged with assuming personal responsibility for the success of the entire project. At Chrysler, for example, the boundaries of the groups within its product development organization historically had been defined by components—power train, electrical systems, and so on. But to accelerate auto development, Chrysler needed to focus not on components but on automobile platforms—the minivan, small car, Jeep, and truck, for example—so it created heavyweight teams. Although these organizational units aren't as good at focusing on component design, they facilitated the definition of new processes that were much faster and more efficient in integrating various subsystems into new car designs. Companies as diverse as Medtronic for its cardiac pacemakers, IBM for its disk drives, and Eli Lilly for its new blockbuster drug Zyprexa have used heavyweight teams as vehicles for creating new processes so they could develop better products faster.

CREATING CAPABILITIES THROUGH A SPINOUT ORGANIZATION

When the mainstream organization's values would render it incapable of allocating resources to an innovation project, the company should spin it out as a new venture. Large organizations cannot be expected to allocate the critical financial and human resources needed to build a strong position in small, emerging markets. And it is very difficult for a company whose cost structure is tailored to compete in high-end markets to be profitable in low-end markets as well. Spinouts are very much in vogue among managers in old-line companies struggling with the question of how to address the Internet. But that's not always appropriate. When a disruptive innovation requires a different cost structure in order to be profitable and competitive, or when the current size of the opportunity is insignificant relative to the growth needs

of the mainstream organization, then—and only then—
is a spinout organization required.

Hewlett-Packard's laser-printer division in Boise,
Idaho, was hugely successful, enjoying high margins and
a reputation for superior product quality. Unfortunately,
its ink-jet project, which represented a disruptive innovation, languished inside the mainstream HP printer
business. Although the processes for developing the two
types of printers were basically the same, there was a difference in values. To thrive in the ink-jet market, HP
needed to be comfortable with lower gross margins and a
smaller market than its laser printers commanded, and it
needed to be willing to embrace relatively lower performance standards. It was not until HP's managers
decided to transfer the unit to a separate division in Van-
couver, British Columbia, with the goal of competing
head-to-head with its own laser business, that the ink-jet
business finally became successful.

How separate does such an effort need to be? A new
physical location isn't always necessary. The primary
requirement is that the project not be forced to compete
for resources with projects in the mainstream organization. As we have seen, projects that are inconsistent with
a company's mainstream values will naturally be
accorded lowest priority. Whether the independent organization is physically separate is less important than its
independence from the normal decision-making criteria
in the resource allocation process. "Fitting the Tool to
the Task" at the end of this article goes into more detail
about what kind of innovation challenge is best met by
which organizational structure.

Managers think that developing a new operation necessarily means abandoning the old one, and they're

loathe to do that since it works perfectly well for what it was designed to do. But when disruptive change appears on the horizon, managers need to assemble the capabilities to confront that change before it affects the mainstream business. They actually need to run two businesses in tandem—one whose processes are tuned to the existing business model and another that is geared toward the new model. Merrill Lynch, for example, has accomplished an impressive global expansion of its institutional financial services through careful execution of its existing planning, acquisition, and partnership processes. Now, however, faced with the on-line world, the company is required to plan, acquire, and form partnerships more rapidly. Does that mean Merrill Lynch should change the processes that have worked so well in its traditional investment-banking business? Doing so would be disastrous, if we consider the question through the lens of our framework. Instead, Merrill should retain the old processes when working with the existing business (there are probably a few billion dollars still to be made under the old business model!) and create additional processes to deal with the new class of problems.

One word of warning: in our studies of this challenge, we have never seen a company succeed in addressing a change that disrupts its mainstream values without the personal, attentive oversight of the CEO—precisely because of the power of values in shaping the normal resource allocation process. Only the CEO can ensure that the new organization gets the required resources and is free to create processes and values that are appropriate to the new challenge. CEOs

Once an acquisition's managers are forced to adopt the buyer's way of doing business, its capabilities will disappear.

who view spinouts as a tool to get disruptive threats off their personal agendas are almost certain to meet with failure. We have seen no exceptions to this rule.

CREATING CAPABILITIES THROUGH ACQUISITIONS

Just as innovating managers need to make separate assessments of the capabilities and disabilities that reside in their company's resources, processes, and values, so must they do the same with acquisitions when seeking to buy capabilities. Companies that successfully gain new capabilities through acquisitions are those that know where those capabilities reside in the acquisition and assimilate them accordingly. Acquiring managers begin by asking, "What created the value that I just paid so dearly for? Did I justify the price because of the acquisition's resources? Or was a substantial portion of its worth created by processes and values?"

If the capabilities being purchased are embedded in an acquired company's processes and values, then the last thing the acquiring manager should do is integrate the acquisition into the parent organization. Integration will vaporize the processes and values of the acquired firm. Once the acquisition's managers are forced to adopt the buyer's way of doing business, its capabilities will disappear. A better strategy is to let the business stand alone and to infuse the parent's resources into the acquired company's processes and values. This approach truly constitutes the acquisition of new capabilities.

If, however, the acquired company's resources were the reason for its success and the primary rationale for the acquisition, then integrating it into the parent can make a lot of sense. Essentially, that means plugging the acquired people, products, technology, and customers into the parent's processes as a way of leveraging the parent's existing capabilities.

The perils of the ongoing DaimlerChrysler merger can be better understood in this light. Chrysler had few esources that could be considered unique. Its recent success in the market was rooted in its processes—particularly in its processes for designing products and

Often, it seems, financial analysts have a better intuition about the value of resources than they do about the value of processes.

integrating the efforts of its subsystem suppliers. What is the best way for Daimler to leverage Chrysler's capabilities? Wall Street is pressuring management to consolidate the two organizations to cut costs. But if the two companies are integrated, the very processes that made Chrysler such an attractive acquisition will likely be compromised.

The situation is reminiscent of IBM's 1984 acquisition of the telecommunications company Rolm. There wasn't anything in Rolm's pool of resources that IBM didn't already have. Rather, it was Rolm's processes for developing and finding new markets for PBX products that mattered. Initially, IBM recognized the value in preserving the informal and unconventional culture of the Rolm organization, which stood in stark contrast to IBM's methodical style. However, in 1987 IBM terminated Rolm's subsidiary status and decided to fully integrate the company into its own corporate structure. IBM's managers soon learned the folly of that decision. When they tried to push Rolm's resources—its products and its customers—through the processes that had been honed in the large-computer business, the Rolm business stumbled badly. And it was impossible for a computer company whose values had been whetted on profit margins of 18% to get excited about products with much lower profit margins. IBM's integration of Rolm destroyed the very source of the deal's original worth. DaimlerChrysler, bowing to the investment community's drumbeat for efficiency savings, now stands on the edge of the same precipice. Often, it seems, financial analysts have a better intuition about the value of resources than they do about the value of processes.

By contrast, Cisco Systems' acquisitions process has worked well because, we would argue, it has kept resources, processes, and values in the right perspective. Between 1993 and 1997, it primarily acquired small companies that were less than two years old, early-stage organizations whose market value was built primarily upon their resources, particularly their engineers and products. Cisco plugged those resources into its own effective development, logistics, manufacturing, and marketing processes and threw away whatever nascent processes and values came with the acquisitions because those weren't what it had paid for. On a couple of occasions when the company acquired a larger, more mature organization—notably its 1996 acquisition of StrataCom—Cisco did not integrate. Rather, it let StrataCom stand alone and infused Cisco's substantial resources into StrataCom's organization to help it grow more rapidly. [3]

M ANAGERS WHOSE ORGANIZATIONS are confronting change must first determine whether they have the resources required to succeed. They then need to ask a separate question: Does the organization have the processes and values it needs to succeed in this new situation? Asking this second question is not as instinctive for most managers because the processes by which work is done and the values by which employees make their decisions have served them well in the past. What we hope this framework introduces into managers' thinking is the idea that the very capabilities that make their organizations effective also define their disabilities. In that regard, a little time spent soul-searching for honest answers to the following questions will pay off handsomely: Are the processes by which work habitually gets done in the organization appropriate for this new problem? And will the values of the organization cause this initiative to get high priority or to languish?

If the answers to those questions are no, it's okay. Understanding a problem is the most crucial step in solving it. Wishful thinking about these issues can set teams that need to innovate on a course fraught with roadblocks, second-guessing, and frustration. The reason that innovation often seems to be so difficult for established companies is that they employ highly capable people and then set them to work within organizational structures whose processes and values weren't designed for the task at hand. Ensuring that capable people are ensconced in capable organizations is a major responsibility of management in a transformational age such as ours.

Digital's Dilemma

A LOT OF BUSINESS THINKERS have analyzed Digital Equipment Corporation's abrupt fall from grace. Most have concluded that Digital simply read the market very badly. But if we look at the company's fate through the lens of our framework, a different picture emerges.

Digital was a spectacularly successful maker of mini-computers from the 1960s through the 1980s. One might have been tempted to assert, when personal computers first appeared in the market around 1980, that Digital's core capability was in building computers. But if that were the case, why did the company stumble?

Clearly, Digital had the resources to succeed in personal computers. Its engineers routinely designed computers that were far more sophisticated than PCs. The company had plenty of cash, a great brand, good technology, and so on. But it did not have the processes to succeed in the personal computer business. Minicomputer companies designed most of the key components of their computers internally and then integrated those components into proprietary configurations. Designing a new product platform took two to three years. Digital manufactured most of its own components and assembled them in a batch mode. It sold directly to corporate engineering organizations. Those processes worked extremely well in the minicomputer business.

PC makers, by contrast, outsourced most components from the best suppliers around the globe. New computer designs, made up of modular components, had to be completed in six to 12 months. The computers were manufactured in high-volume assembly lines and sold through retailers to consumers and businesses. None of these processes existed within Digital. In other words, although the people working at the company had the ability to design, build, and sell personal computers profitably, they were working in an organization that was incapable of doing so because its processes had been designed and had evolved to do other tasks well.

Similarly, because of its overhead costs, Digital had to adopt a set of values that dictated, "If it generates 50% gross margins or more, it's good business. If it generates less than 40% margins, it's not worth doing." Management had to ensure that all employees gave priority to projects according to these criteria or the company couldn't make money. Because PCs generated lower margins, they did not fit with Digital's values. The company's criteria for setting priorities always placed higher-performance minicomputers ahead of personal computers in the resource-allocation process.

Digital could have created a different organization that would have honed the different processes and values required to succeed in PCs—as IBM did. But Digital's mainstream organization simply was incapable of succeeding at the job.

Fitting the Tool to the Task

SUPPOSE THAT AN ORGANIZATION NEEDS to react to or initiate an innovation. The matrix illustrated below can help managers understand what kind of team should work on the project and what organizational structure that team needs to work within. The vertical axis asks the manager to measure the extent to which the organization's existing processes are suited to getting the new job done effectively. The horizontal axis asks managers to assess whether the organization's values will permit the company to allocate the resources the new initiative needs.

In region A, the project is a good fit with the company's processes and values, so no new capabilities are called for. A functional or a lightweight team can tackle the project within the existing organizational structure. A functional team works on function-specific issues, then passes the project on to the next function. A lightweight team is cross-functional, but team members stay under the control of their respective functional managers.

In region B, the project is a good fit with the company's values but not with its processes. It presents the organization with new types of problems and therefore requires new types of interactions and coordination among groups and individuals. The team, like the team in region A, is working on a sustaining rather than a disruptive innovation. In this case, a heavyweight team is a good bet, but the project can be executed within the mainstream company. A heavyweight team—whose members work solely on the project and are expected to behave like general managers, shouldering responsibility for the project's success—is designed so that new processes and new ways of working together can emerge.

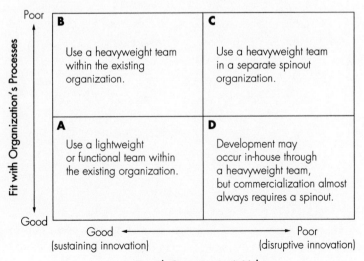

Fit with Organization's Processes

Poor → Good

B
Use a heavyweight team within the existing organization.

C
Use a heavyweight team in a separate spinout organization.

A
Use a lightweight or functional team within the existing organization.

D
Development may occur in-house through a heavyweight team, but commercialization almost always requires a spinout.

Good (sustaining innovation) ← → Poor (disruptive innovation)

Fit with Organization's Values

In region C, the manager faces a disruptive change that doesn't fit the organization's existing processes or values. To ensure success, the manager should create a spinout organization and commission a heavyweight development team to tackle the challenge. The spinout will allow the project to be governed by different values—a different cost structure, for example, with lower profit margins. The heavyweight team (as in region B) will ensure that new processes can emerge.

Similarly, in region D, when a manager faces a disruptive change that fits the organization's current processes but doesn't fit its values, the key to success almost always lies in commissioning a heavyweight development team to work in a spinout. Development may occasionally happen successfully in-house, but successful commercialization will require a spinout.

Unfortunately, most companies employ a one-size-fits-all organizing strategy, using lightweight or functional teams for programs of every size and character. But such teams are tools for exploiting established capabilities. And among those few companies that have accepted the heavyweight gospel, many have attempted to organize *all* of their development teams in a heavyweight fashion. Ideally, each company should tailor the team structure and organizational location to the process and values required by each project.

Notes

1. See Dorothy Leonard-Barton, "Core Capabilities and Core Rigidities: A Paradox in Managing New Product Development," *Strategic Management Journal* (summer, 1992).

2. Our description of the development of an organization's culture draws heavily from Edgar Schein's research, as first laid out in his book *Organizational Culture and Leadership* (Jossey-Bass Publishers, 1985).

3. See Charles A. Holloway, Stephen C. Wheelwright, and Nicole Tempest, "Cisco Systems, Inc.: Post-Acquisition Manufacturing Integration," a case published jointly by the Stanford and Harvard Business Schools, 1998.

Originally published in March–April 2000
Reprint R00202

Discovering New Points of Differentiation

IAN C. MACMILLAN AND
RITA GUNTHER MCGRATH

Executive Summary

MOST PROFITABLE STRATEGIES are built on differentiation: offering customers something they value that competitors don't have. But most companies concentrate only on their products or services. In fact, a company can differentiate itself at every point where it comes in contact with its customers—from the moment customers realize they need a product or service to the time when they dispose of it. The authors believe that if companies open up their thinking to their customers' entire experience with a product or service—the *consumption chain*—they can uncover opportunities to position their offerings in ways that neither they nor their competitors thought possible.

The authors show how even a mundane product such as candles can be successfully differentiated. By analyzing its customers' experiences and exploring various options, Blyth Industries, for example, has grown from a

$2 million U.S. candle manufacturer into a global candle and accessory business with nearly $500 million in sales and a market value of $1.2 billion.

Finding ways to differentiate one's company is a skill that can be nurtured, the authors contend. In this Manager's Tool Kit, they have designed a two-part approach that can help companies continually identify new points of differentiation and develop the ability to generate successful differentiation strategies. "Mapping the Consumption Chain" captures the customer's total experience with a product or service. "Analyzing Your Customer's Experience" shows managers how directed brainstorming about each step in the consumption chain can elicit numerous ways to differentiate any offering.

MOST PROFITABLE STRATEGIES are built on differentiation: offering customers something they value that competitors don't have. But most companies, in seeking to differentiate themselves, focus their energy only on their products or services. In fact, a company has the opportunity to differentiate itself at every point where it comes in contact with its customers—from the moment customers realize that they need a product or service to the time when they no longer want it and decide to dispose of it. We believe that if companies open up their creative thinking to their customers' entire experience with a product or service—what we call the *consumption chain*—they can uncover opportunities to position their offerings in ways that they, and their competitors, would never have thought possible.

Take the case of Blyth Industries, a candle manufacturer. By differentiating and redifferentiating its products, Blyth has been able to grow from a $2 million U.S. producer of candles used for religious purposes to a global candle and accessory business with nearly $500 million in sales and a market value of $1.2 billion. Not bad for a company in an industry that, as CEO Robert B. Goergen says, "has been in decline for 300 years." Blyth's story is, quite simply, a manifestation of the power of strategic differentiation.

Business history is full of stories of entrepreneurs who stumbled upon a great idea that then became the cornerstone of a successful company. But finding ways to differentiate one's company doesn't have to be an act of genius or intuition. It is a skill that can be developed and nurtured. We have designed a two-part approach that can help companies continually identify new points of differentiation and develop the ability to generate successful differentiation strategies. The first part, "Mapping the Consumption Chain," captures the customer's total experience with a product or service. The second, "Analyzing Your Customer's Experience," shows managers how directed brainstorming about each step in the consumption chain can elicit numerous ways to differentiate even the most mundane product or service.

Mapping the Consumption Chain

As we've said, the first step toward strategic differentiation is to map your customer's entire experience with your product or service. We recommend that companies perform this exercise for each important customer segment.

To begin, assemble groups from all areas of your company—in particular, those employees who use marketing data and those who have face-to-face or phone contact with customers. Charge the groups with identifying, for each major market segment, all the steps through which customers pass from the time they first become aware of your product to the time when they finally have to dispose of it or discontinue using it.

The first step is to map your customer's entire experience with a product.

Naturally, every product or service will have a somewhat different consumption chain. However, a few activities are common to most chains. Consider the following questions, each of which illustrates one of those activities. Then, as the group begins to get a feel for the special relationship between your customers and your products, ask questions about more complex activities that pertain to your business.

HOW DO PEOPLE BECOME AWARE OF THEIR NEED FOR YOUR PRODUCT OR SERVICE?

Are consumers aware that you can satisfy their need? Are they aware that they even have a need that can be satisfied? Your company can create a powerful source of differentiation if it can make consumers aware of a need in a way that is unique and subtle.

Consider the problem of differentiating an everyday consumer product, such as a toothbrush. For many people, brushing is a ritual to which they pay relatively little attention. As a consequence, many brushes are used well past the point when their bristles are worn and are no longer effective. Toothbrush maker Oral-B discovered a way to capitalize on this widespread habit. The company, by introducing a patented blue dye in the center bristles of its toothbrushes, found a way to have the brush itself communicate to the customer. As the brush is used, the dye gradually fades. When the dye is gone, the brush is no longer effective and should be replaced. Customers are thus made aware of a need that previously had gone unrecognized. So far, the idea sounds like something out of Marketing 101. What gives it particular value is that the need can be filled *only* by Oral-B's patented process. The company turned differentiation into a competitive advantage.

HOW DO CONSUMERS FIND YOUR OFFERING?

Opportunities for differentiating on the basis of the search process include making your product available when others are not (24-hour telephone-order lines), offering your product in places where competitors do not offer theirs (the mini McDonald's outlets in Wal-Mart stores), and making your product ubiquitous (Coca-Cola). Making the search process less complicated, more convenient, less expensive, and more habitual are all ways in which companies can differentiate themselves. And when competitors can't or won't do the same—at least, not right away—you have the potential for a strategic advantage.

One example is the rapid growth of catalog sales in channels formerly dominated by retail chains. Consumers now can obtain detailed, up-to-the-minute information about a breathtaking range of products over the telephone or through the Internet, without enduring the inconvenience of visiting a showroom and the often inadequate knowledge of the floor sales staff. The PC

Connection & Mac Connection, a company that sells computers through its catalog, operates a 24-hour-a-day, seven-day-a-week toll-free phone number for people wanting information about *Can you make the buying process more convenient and less irritating?* computers, software, and related products. When a caller expresses an interest in buying a computer system, a company representative asks a set of questions to narrow down the possibilities to a few good candidates. The rep and the consumer then can discuss each option in detail. What is remarkable about this approach is that, in effect, it allows consumers to tailor the search experience to their own needs.

HOW DO CONSUMERS MAKE THEIR FINAL SELECTIONS?

After a consumer has narrowed down the possibilities, he or she must make a choice. Can you make the selection process more comfortable, less irritating, or more convenient? Look for the *CarMax and AutoNation "sell" cars by letting customers create their own selection process.* ideal situation, in which competitors' procedures actually discourage people from selecting their products, while your procedures encourage people to come to you. Citibank for years captured a significant share of the college student market for credit cards simply by making it easy for students to obtain a card while competitors made it difficult.

Another example of this dynamic is playing out right now in the used-car business. For many potential customers, the experience of choosing a used car is an ordeal—to the point where one CEO of a major automaker observed that some people would rather have a root canal. But a new method of selecting cars is transforming the industry. Companies such as CarMax Auto Superstore and AutoNation USA have targeted the selection experience as their competitive focus. At a CarMax showroom, customers sit in front of a computer and specify what features they are looking for in an automobile. They can then, in private, scroll through detailed descriptions of cars that might meet their needs. The final (and only) price for each vehicle is listed. A sales assistant then lets the customers inspect the autos that interest them and handles all the paperwork if they decide to buy one. The "selling" is done not by the salespeople but by the selection process the customers create for themselves.

HOW DO CUSTOMERS ORDER AND PURCHASE YOUR PRODUCT OR SERVICE?

This question is particularly important for relatively low-cost, high-volume items. Can a company differentiate itself by making the process of ordering and purchasing more convenient?

American Hospital Supply revolutionized its industry by radically simplifying the ordering and restocking process for such products as bandages, tongue depressors, syringes, and disinfectants. The company installed computer terminals at each hospital and medical supply store with which it did business. The terminals connected those customers directly to the company's system, allowing direct drop shipment and automatic restocking whenever supplies fell below a certain level. Hallmark uses a similar approach for its greeting cards.

Many companies, including ice-cream makers and pet-food manufacturers, are also using this method to stock supermarket shelves, reaping the benefits of preferred access to these crucial outlets as well as of superior displays. Another, more subtle benefit of this form of differentiation is that it imposes a switching cost on customers that might be tempted to try another supplier. Once customers have signed on, it is expensive for them to switch; this deterrent creates a barrier to competition and, once again, a potential strategic advantage for the supplier.

HOW IS YOUR PRODUCT OR SERVICE DELIVERED?

Delivery affords many opportunities for differentiation, especially if the product is an impulse purchase or if the customer needs it immediately. Let's return to our catalog computer dealer, the PC Connection. Customers can call its toll-free number as late as 3 A.M. to receive "next-day" shipments of items in stock. How does the company do it? The amazing turnaround times are possible because the warehousing and distribution facilities are conveniently located near an Airborne Express hub. Packages can be picked up at the warehouse, transferred to Airborne, and shipped to the customer in a matter of hours. Not only does this delivery strategy constitute a real benefit for customers, but, because there are a limited number of opportunities for such a warehouse-hub connection, competitors will find it hard to adopt the same strategy.

WHAT HAPPENS WHEN YOUR PRODUCT OR SERVICE IS DELIVERED?

An often overlooked opportunity for differentiation lies in considering what has to happen from the time a company delivers a product to the time the customer actually uses it. Opening, inspecting, transporting, and assembling products are frequently major issues for customers.

That applies even to the delivery of services. Consider how difficult it can be to get an auto accident claim processed and paid by an insurance company. Now consider how Progressive Insurance of Cleveland, Ohio, tackled the problem. The company has a fleet of claims adjusters on the road every day, ready to rush to the scene of any auto accident in their territory. There they can record all the information they need and often settle claims on the spot for policyholders. The process has greatly increased customer satisfaction by eliminating the hassle and delay that so often accompany conventional reporting, inspection, and assessment methods. A side benefit for the company is that its approach also has decreased the incidence of fraud by reducing the opportunity to file false claims and inflate repair bills.

HOW IS YOUR PRODUCT INSTALLED?

This step in the consumption chain is particularly relevant for companies with complex products. For example, installation has presented an enormous barrier for computer manufacturers trying to break into the novice-PC-user market. Computer beginners are notoriously intolerant of such on-screen messages as "Disk Error 23."

Compaq Computer, with its Presario line, was among the first to target installation as a source of differentiation. Instead of providing an instruction book filled with technical terminology, Compaq offers its customers a poster that clearly illustrates the ten installation steps. The company uses color-coded cords, cables, and outlets to simplify installation further and also has rigged its computers so that a cheerful video and audio presentation leads new users through the setup and registration process when they first turn on the machine.

HOW IS YOUR PRODUCT OR SERVICE PAID FOR?

Many companies unwittingly cause their customers major difficulties with their payment policies. Here's a test to see whether payment might be such an issue for your customers: Take a walk over to your accounts-receivable department and ask to see a copy of a recent invoice. If your company is anything like about 80% of those we have worked with, the invoice will be virtually incomprehensible. Why? Because invoices are generally designed by systems people for systems, not customers. Given the prevalence of this situation, your company may find opportunities to set itself apart by making the whole payment process easier for customers to understand.

You may discover even greater opportunities by rethinking why your company uses its current payment policy in the first place. We once worked with a company in the energy control business that was having a hard time selling its services to residential co-op owners. At every co-op, the company ran into opposition from a hard core of owners who resisted the capital outlay involved in installing an energy management system. The company eventually won a huge share of the co-op market by altering its policy. Customers no longer pay an up-front installation fee; instead, they pay over time, out of the energy savings.

HOW IS YOUR PRODUCT STORED?

When it is expensive, inconvenient, or downright dangerous for customers to have a product simply sitting around, the opportunities for differentiation abound. Air Products and Chemicals, a producer of industrial gases, grew to dominate its market segments by addressing the problem of storage. Realizing that most of its customers—chemical companies—would rather avoid the burden of having to store vast quantities of dangerous high-pressure gases, Air Products built small industrial-gas plants next to customers' sites. The move pleased customers; it also generated switching costs. Best of all, once an Air Products plant was in place, competitors had little opportunity to move in.

HOW IS YOUR PRODUCT MOVED AROUND?

What difficulties do customers encounter when they must transport a product from one location to another? Whether the journey is across a room or across a state, this step in the consumption chain is another often-overlooked opportunity for differentiation. Ask yourself the following questions: Does the customer find the product fragile? Difficult to package? Awkward to move?

Consider how John Sculley's marketing team at Pepsi-Cola used packaging as a way to differentiate Pepsi from Coke. Sculley's team created a distinct—if temporary—advantage for Pepsi in the early 1970s by designing plastic bottles that were lighter, and thus easier for customers to carry, than the heavy glass bottles of the time. The beauty of the move was that it not only made carrying soda easier, but it also reduced the advantage of Coke's well-known contoured glass bottle. At the time, it was difficult to produce plastic bottles in that shape.

WHAT IS THE CUSTOMER REALLY USING YOUR PRODUCT FOR?

Finding better ways for customers to use a product or service is a powerful differentiator. And such opportunities abound, especially for companies whose products are expensive and used relatively infrequently. General Electric's Transportation Systems division, which manufactures diesel-electric locomotives, used this step in the consumption chain as the basis for rethinking its business.

With few exceptions, the railroads that are the customers for GE's locomotives are not all that attached to a particular unit. What they really want to know is, if they have freight to ship, will a locomotive be there to haul it? GE is working on an arrangement through which the company will guarantee that a locomotive will be available on demand. Under that arrangement, GE will take over the management of all the engines in the customer's system. It will relieve the customer of repair and maintenance concerns, and also will gain economies of scale by managing an entire network. What's more, the entry barrier created by such a system can be formidable.

WHAT DO CUSTOMERS NEED HELP WITH WHEN THEY USE YOUR PRODUCT?

The company with the most helpful response has a significant advantage here. GE, for instance, has an enormously popular 800 number that is available 24 hours a day to help people who have difficulty using any of the company's consumer products. Similarly, Butterball Turkey's 24-hour hot line fields cooking questions from hundreds of customers every Thanksgiving. Butterball has recently supplemented its hot line with an Internet home page and a turkey-cooking guide that its customers can download.

WHAT ABOUT RETURNS OR EXCHANGES?

Too many companies put all their efforts into the selling side of the product life cycle, forgetting that long-term loyalty requires attention to customers' needs throughout their experience with a product. Handling things well when the product doesn't work out can be as powerful as meeting the need that motivated the initial purchase.

Nordstrom is an excellent example of a company that has taken this issue to heart. The clothing retailer captured national publicity in the 1970s when one of its store managers "took back" a set of tires from a customer despite the fact that Nordstrom did not sell tires. By focusing on and aggressively promoting its no-questions-asked return policy, Nordstrom has enhanced its position as a company that provides unique customer service. Customers may be unhappy with the brands they return, but they are not unhappy with the store.

HOW IS YOUR PRODUCT REPAIRED OR SERVICED?

As many users of high-tech products will attest, repair experiences—both good and bad—can influence a lifetime of subsequent purchases.

An ideal solution, used by Tandem Computers—a company that makes computers with parallel central-processing units for applications in which downtime is a major problem—is to try to repair a product even before the customer is aware that such service is needed. Tandem staff members can spot a malfunctioning component through remote diagnostics, send the appropriate part and instructions to the customer by express mail, and walk the customer through the repair process on the phone. This approach has almost completely eliminated expensive and inconvenient downtime for the company's customers; it also has eliminated their need for a costly on-site service force.

Otis Elevator uses remote diagnostics in a different way. In high-traffic office buildings, where servicing elevators is a major inconvenience to occupants and visitors alike, Otis uses its remote-diagnostics capabilities to predict possible service interruptions. It sends employees to carry out preventive maintenance in the evening, when traffic is light.

WHAT HAPPENS WHEN YOUR PRODUCT IS DISPOSED OF OR NO LONGER USED?

In a world in which it is becoming increasingly economical simply to replace many products as they age rather than spend the money to fix them, what do customers do with the obsolete goods?

Canon offers an interesting example of how a company can differentiate itself at this step in the chain. It has developed a system that allows customers to return spent printer cartridges at Canon's expense. The cartridges are then rehabilitated and resold as such. The process makes it easy for customers to return used cartridges: all they need to do is drop the prepaid package off at a United Parcel Service collection station. At the same time, it enhances the image of Canon as an environmentally friendly organization.

Analyzing Your Customer's Experience

Although mapping the consumption chain is a useful tool in itself, the strategic value of our approach lies in the next step: analyzing your customer's experience. The objective is to gain insight into the customer by appreciating the context within which each step of the consumption chain unfolds. It is crucial to remember that the customer is always interacting with people, places, occasions, or activities. Those interactions determine the customer's feelings toward your product or service at each link in the chain. When they are viewed strategically, they can shape the dynamics of competition for that customer's business.

To analyze your customer's experience, consider how five simple questions apply at each link in the chain.

Essentially, this step involves considering how a series of simple questions—*what, where, who, when,* and *how*—apply at each link in the consumption chain. We have found that the most rewarding way to approach this exercise is to have a group of people from a company start down a path with any of their questions and brainstorm until their ideas dry up. Sometimes a given question will not lead to any particular insight. That's not a problem; the goal is to assemble an inventory of possible points of differentiation. Once the ideas are on the table, you can assess each one and select those that are most promising for your situation.

Blyth Industries, the candle manufacturer we mentioned earlier, provides a good example of how analyzing your customer's experience works in practice. By exploring the options raised by their analysis, Blyth employees were able to take a prosaic product that is easy to imitate and create a profitable competitive advantage. What is important to understand here is that Blyth makes no pretense of being able to create the fabled "sustained competitive advantage"—so beloved of strategy texts—in any single segment of the candle market. Rather, what the company seeks to do is be the first to create and then dominate many small niches in rapid succession over time, gaining economies of distribution and scale by the sheer number of products it has in the marketplace.

Consider some of the possibilities that Blyth employees uncovered when they applied the questions to their business:

WHAT?

What are customers doing at each point in the consumption chain? What else would they like to be doing? What problems could they be experiencing? (These problems may not be directly related to your product or service.) Is there anything you can do to enhance their experience while they are at this stage of the chain?

Candle makers might explore the possibility of offering a complete "candlelight experience."

Candles, when you think about it, can play a role in everyday life in a host of different ways. Among other things, they are used to celebrate birthdays, create a festive atmosphere for dinner parties, warm buffet dishes, cope with power outages, and set the mood for romantic evenings. Candles can be purchased in specialty shops, at crafts fairs, in supermarkets, and at card stores. Further, their use can be accompanied by a huge variety of containers, displays, accents, and mood-creating products. All this suggests that candle makers might do well to explore the possibility of offering a complete "candlelight experience" by producing or marketing complementary products as well.

WHERE?

Where are your customers when they are at this point in the consumption chain? Where else might they be? Where would they like to be? Can you arrange for them to be there? Do they have any concerns about their location?

Because candles can have so many uses, it isn't surprising that there are as many potential places for their use. Candles can be found at the beach, on picnics, at proms, at weddings, at home, in restaurants, at children's birthday parties, and in places of worship. What quickly became evident to Blyth was that the concerns and behavior patterns of its customers were likely to be different in each location. That insight suggested the potential for differentiation on the basis of location.

For example, consider how candles are used in the home. Virtually every room in the house has potential: the dining room, living room, kitchen, bedroom, bathroom, and basement can all conceivably provide a setting for candle use, each for a different reason.

WHO?

Who else is with the customer at any given link in the chain? Do those other people have any influence over the customer? Are their thoughts or concerns important? If

you could arrange it, who else might be with the customer? If you could arrange it, how might those other
people influence the customer's decision to buy your
product?

Honing in on the line of thinking Blyth used about
domestic candles, consider the use of candles in the dining room. Who else is going to be there? The other people could be members of the immediate or extended
family, business associates, close friends, or a suitor.
Each type of person means a possible point of differentiation; each type means a different experience, a different
mood, and a different time.

WHEN?

When—at what time of day or night, on what day of the
week, at what time of the year—are your customers at
any given link in the chain? Does this timing cause any
problems? If you could arrange it, when would they be at
this link?

Take the scenario of a dining room with the family.
Blyth found that the question *when* uncovered a wealth
of opportunities for differentiation. Candles are used in
the dining room with the family on birthdays, anniver-
saries, holidays, and graduation days, and at meals mark-
ing other special occasions. Each occasion provides a distinct experience. Important for a candle maker, each also
triggers distinct emotions. Blyth employees were able to
identify what became several successful new areas of differentiation by exploring how their candles might be
designed in special shapes, colors, or scents. They also
came up with a variety of ways to package the candles
and combine them with such accessories as napkins to
suit each situation. Candles intended for use with family
members at Thanksgiving, for example, might be scented

with cinnamon, colored in tones associated with the holiday, and sold with special holders.

Because there are many holidays and other occasions when families get together in the dining room, you can begin to get a sense of the opportunities available for differentiation. Moreover, the process can be repeated for as many different companions and settings as the imagination of your employees can contemplate. Blyth, for

Even a simple product such as gasoline can be differentiated.

example, also has found a tremendous opportunity to differentiate its products for romantic meals. CEO Goergen has worked hard to design

scented candles in various shapes in order to influence the ambience of such occasions so that, as he says, "eating becomes dining, and dining becomes romance."

HOW?

How are your customers' needs being addressed? Do they have any concerns about the way in which your company is meeting their needs? How else might you attend to their needs and concerns?

Think about how candles are used outdoors—say, at a company barbecue. Citronella candles come to mind. In addition to creating a festive atmosphere, they are an attractive way to protect people from insect bites.

As we've seen, there is considerable potential for differentiation even in products so simple that at first blush they seem like commodities. Candles are but one. Gasoline is another. (See "Is There a Way to Differentiate Selling Gas?" at the end of this article.) Understanding the customer's experience at any link in the chain for any product offers companies the opportunity to identify and explore many nontraditional ways to create value. The task then becomes selecting from among this wealth of possibilities; considering how each idea meshes with a company's particular skills, assets, and systems; and focusing only on those that can generate a competitive advantage.

Consider how each idea meshes with your company's skills, assets, and systems.

Each idea also may open up an opportunity to develop a new competence.

Too many companies pursue what seem like great new ideas without carefully assessing whether their organizations are well suited to do so and how quickly competitors can respond. Robert Goergen knows that Blyth Industries has certain strengths its competitors do not, including several unique production techniques and, more important, a deep knowledge of fragrances. Those special strengths, coupled with a solid understanding of customers based on market research, give Blyth an edge. Goergen thus evaluates opportunities for differentiation based on those considerations and moves forward only with the ideas that promise the strongest returns.

Focused Creativity

Virtually every company we have ever worked with has within it scores of people of considerable creativity and imagination. Unfortunately, all too often, the company never benefits because that talent isn't appropriately focused. It may even be squelched by the homogenizing pressures that any large organization tends to impose.

An important benefit of the process we've outlined above is that it unlocks the creativity in an organization so that the insights of particular individuals can contribute to a shared understanding of the customer—so that the company, in effect, knows its customers almost better than they know themselves. Companies that do this successfully find themselves deeply attuned to their markets. And, like entrepreneurs, they spend the imagination they have in lieu of the money they may lack to outperform competitors where it counts.

Is There a Way to Differentiate Selling Gas?

CONSIDER THE "PURCHASE LINK" of the consumption chain.

If you pursue the business-trip option, the next question is,
Whom are they with when they buy gasoline on a business trip?
Your customer could be alone or accompanied by a colleague. He or she could be with a spouse or significant other. Your customer also could be traveling with a group of people.

What else are your customers doing when they buy gasoline?
Among other things, they might be commuting, on a leisure trip, on a business trip, on vacation, shopping, or planning to use equipment (such as a mower or a tiller).

If you pursue the idea that your customer is alone, the next question is,
Where does your customer buy gasoline while he or she is on the business trip?
Your customer might stop first at a local gas station, then again between cities along the way.

Which leads to:
Does your customer have any concerns in any of those situations, and how is your company addressing them?

Among other things, your customer might worry about getting lost or running out of gas. Or he or she might be concerned about personal security. Also, your customer certainly doesn't want the car to break down.

Keeping those ideas in mind, consider:

When does your customer buy gasoline?

Anytime: during the day or night; during the week or on the weekend.

If you consider in depth the concern about personal security, one way to differentiate the process of selling gasoline would be to reconfigure the structure of your gas stations along those highways that are principal business routes. For example, you could

- ensure that your station is well lit and monitored;

- provide an attendant to pump the gas;

- provide a "travel adviser" at each station who has a detailed knowledge of the area; such a person might be able to advise your customer about the safest routes, areas under construction, congested areas, and good restaurants and hotels;

- arrange for customers who buy gas to rent a mobile phone at the gas station, possibly negotiating with the phone company to share usage revenues.

Originally published in July–August 1997
Reprint 97408

From Spare Change to Real Change

The Social Sector as Beta Site for Business Innovation

ROSABETH MOSS KANTER

Executive Summary

CORPORATIONS ARE CONTINUALLY LOOKING for new sources of innovation. Today several leading companies are beginning to find inspiration in an unexpected place: the social sector. That includes public schools, welfare-to-work programs, and the inner city.

Indeed, a new paradigm for innovation is emerging: a partnership between private enterprise and public interest that produces profitable and sustainable change for both sides.

In this article, the author shows how some companies are moving beyond corporate social responsibility to corporate social innovation. Traditionally, companies viewed the social sector as a dumping ground for their spare cash, obsolete equipment, and tired executives. But that mind-set hardly created lasting change. Now companies are viewing community needs as opportunities to develop ideas and demonstrate business technologies, find and serve new markets; and solve long-standing business problems. They focus on inventing sophisticated solutions through a hands-on approach. This is not charity; it is R & D, a strategic business investment.

The author concedes that it isn't easy to make the new paradigm work. But she has found that successful private-public partnerships share six characteristics: a clear business agenda, strong partners committed to change, investment by both parties, rootedness in the user community, links to other organizations, and a commitment to sustain and replicate the results. Drawing on examples of successful companies such as IBM and Bell Atlantic, the author illustrates how this paradigm has produced innovations that have both business and community payoffs.

Winning in business today demands innovation. Companies that innovate reap all the advantages of a first mover. They acquire a deep knowledge of new markets and develop strong relationships within them. Innovators also build a reputation of being able to solve the most challenging problems. That's why corporations spend billions of dollars each year trying to identify opportunities for innovation—unsolved problems or unmet needs, things that don't fit or don't work. They set up learning laboratories where they can stretch their thinking, extend their capabilities, experiment with new technologies, get feedback from early users about product potential, and gain experience working with underserved and emerging markets.

Today several leading companies are beginning to find inspiration in an unexpected place: the social sector—in public schools, welfare-to-work programs, and the inner city. These companies have discovered that social problems are economic problems, whether it is the need for a trained workforce or the search for new markets in neglected parts of cities. They have learned

Companies view community needs as opportunities to develop ideas, serve new markets, and solve long-standing business problems.

that applying their energies to solving the chronic problems of the social sector powerfully stimulates their own business development. Today's better-educated children are tomorrow's knowledge workers. Lower unemployment in the inner city means higher consumption in the inner city. Indeed, a new paradigm for innovation is emerging: a partnership between private enterprise and public interest that produces profitable and sustainable change for both sides.

The new paradigm is long overdue. Traditional solutions to America's recalcitrant social ills amount to little more than Band-Aids. Consider the condition of public education. Despite an estimated 200,000 business partnerships with public schools, fundamental aspects of public education have barely changed in decades. And performance is still weak. There are two reasons for this. First, traditional corporate volunteer activities only scratch the surface. And second, companies often just throw money at the problem, then walk away. The fact is, many recipients of business largesse often don't need charity; they need change. Not spare change, but real change—sustainable, replicable, institutionalized change that transforms their schools, their job prospects, and their neighborhoods. And that means getting business deeply involved in nontraditional ways.

Doing Good by Doing Well

My team of researchers and I have found a number of companies that are breaking the mold—they are moving beyond corporate social *responsibility* to corporate social *innovation.* These companies are the vanguard of the new paradigm. They view community needs as opportunities to develop ideas and demonstrate business technologies, to find and serve new markets, and to solve long-standing business problems. They focus their efforts on inventing sophisticated solutions through a hands-on approach. (See "Why America Needs Corporate Social Innovation" at the end of this article.)

Tackling social sector problems forces companies to stretch their capabilities to produce innovations that have business as well as community payoffs. When companies approach social needs in this way, they have a stake in the problems, and they treat the effort the way they would treat any other project central to the company's operations. They use their best people and their core skills. This is not charity; it is R&D—a strategic business investment. Let's look at a few examples from the fields of education, welfare programs, and inner-city development.

PUBLIC EDUCATION

In 1991, Bell Atlantic began creating one of the first-ever models for using computer networks in public schools.

Bell Atlantic's Project Explore, in Union City, New Jersey, enabled communication and learning to move beyond the classroom. In addition to installing computers in the schools, Bell Atlantic gave computers to 135 inner-city students and their teachers to use at home. Project Explore became a catalyst for increasing the use of technology to transform middle- and high-school classrooms, to improve students' skills, and to involve parents in their children's education. Union City's schools, once threatened with state takeover, have become national role models. For its part, Bell Atlantic has found new ways of handling data transmission. It refined its goals for video on demand and identified a new market in distance learning.

IBM began its Reinventing Education program in 1994 under the personal leadership of CEO Louis V. Gerstner, Jr. Today the program, designed to develop new tools and solutions for systemic change, operates in 21 U.S. sites and in four other countries. Many product innovations, which benefit both the schools and IBM, have resulted from this initiative. As part of the Wired for Learning program in four new schools in Charlotte-Mecklenburg, North Carolina, for example, IBM created tools to connect parents to teachers digitally so that parents can view their children's schoolwork from home or a community center and compare it with the district's academic standard. New tracking software is facilitating the introduction of flexible scheduling in Cincinnati, Ohio, including in a new year-round high school. In Broward County, Florida—the fifth largest school district in the United States—IBM's data-warehousing technology gives teachers and administrators access to extensive information on students. In Philadelphia, Pennsylvania, IBM created a voice recognition tool to teach reading, which is based on children's high-pitched voices and speech patterns.

WELFARE-TO-WORK PROGRAMS

Since 1991, the hotel group Marriott International has been refining its pioneering training program, Pathways to Independence. The program, which currently runs in 13 U.S. cities, hones the job skills, life skills, and work habits of welfare recipients, and Marriott guarantees participants a job offer when they complete the program. The challenges of working with the unemployed has led the company to new insights about training, job placement, and supervision, which have helped Marriott reap the benefits of a more stable workforce and maintain unusually high standards of service. Pathways was a radical improvement on traditional programs for the hard to employ, which were both bureaucratically cumbersome and often ineffective. The employee assistance innovations that Marriott has developed through the program have also created new jobs in poor communities.

United Airlines is another company that derives business benefits from tapping a new workforce. Taking a leadership role in the Welfare-to-Work Partnership (a national coalition of 8,000 businesses that have pledged to hire people off the welfare rolls), CEO Gerald Greenwald seeks new ways to transport people from inner cities to suburban jobs. United has also created human resources innovations, such as a new mentoring program. These innovations, developed in collaboration with workers, have become models for the new personnel practices United is now planning to roll out to its more than 10,000 new hires.

INNER-CITY DEVELOPMENT

BankBoston launched First Community Bank in 1990 as a way to target newcomers to the banking system— many of whom were located in the inner city. This initiative also responded to regulatory pressures on banks to increase investment in underserved urban neighborhoods. Thanks to First Community Bank, access to high-quality financial services for disadvantaged minorities and inner-city inhabitants has radically improved, which is helping to revitalize deteriorating neighborhoods.

A company has a better chance of making a difference if it knows how its business agenda relates to specific social needs.

Since its inception, First Community Bank has been a laboratory for a stream of innovations that have been applied across BankBoston. From BankBoston's perspective, First Community Bank has been an undeniable success. The bank has grown from its initial 7 branches in Boston to 42 branches across New England. It offers a range of products and services that includes consumer lending, real estate, small-business loans, and venture capital. Today it is the anchor for all community-banking services within BankBoston.

Making Partnerships Work

Making the new paradigm work isn't easy. In contrast to typical business-to-business relationships, there is an added layer of complexity. Government and nonprofit organizations are driven by goals other than profitability, and they may even be suspicious of business motivations. Additionally, the institutional infrastructure of the social sector is undeveloped in business terms. For that reason, public schools and inner cities can be said to resemble emerging markets. Those difficulties, however, can be overcome. My research has identified six characteristics of successful private-public partnerships: a clear business agenda, strong partners committed to change, investment by both parties, rootedness in the user community, links to other community organizations, and a long-term commitment to sustain and replicate the results.

A CLEAR BUSINESS AGENDA

In the new paradigm, companies obviously want to make a social contribution. But a corporation has a better chance of making a real difference if it knows clearly, in advance, how its business agenda relates to specific social needs. A company that wants to develop new data analysis technology, for example, might target a large and complex education system as its beta site. Finding test users in the public schools would clearly benefit both the community and the company. Indeed, apart from the social benefits, there are two distinct business advantages. The first is the opportunity to test the new technology, and the second is the chance to build political capital—for instance, to influence regulations, to reshape public institutions on which the company depends, to augment a public image as a leader, or to build closer relationships with government officials.

This coincidence of social needs with business and political goals is precisely illustrated by Bell Atlantic's Project Explore. Bell Atlantic was developing intelligent network technologies, video on demand, and other communications ideas. By the early 1990s, Bell Atlantic was

ready to test High-bit-rate Digital Subscriber Line
(HDSL) technologies with personal computers. Bell
Communications Research, then the R&D laboratory
shared by the Baby Bells after their divestiture from
AT&T, sent Bell Atlantic a proposal to equip schools
with computers. That would get the technology out into
the field and allow the company to test the services that
could be delivered over high-capacity lines into schools
and homes.

Working with schools also fit the company's political
agenda. In New Jersey, Bell Atlantic leaders hoped to win
the support of legislators and regulators for the Opportunity New Jersey project, Bell Atlantic's proposed
statewide technology communications plan. To garner
support, they needed a demonstration site to showcase
their communications networks. Bell Atlantic saw that
testing its transmission technology in special-needs
school districts could benefit both the company and the
schools. Bell Atlantic's new technology, however, could
work only for distances of about 9,000 feet on copper
telephone wires, which in New Jersey had not yet been
replaced with fiber-optic lines. The density of Union
City's population and Union City's proximity to Bell
Atlantic's central switching office made it an ideal site
for testing and developing the company's innovations.

Marriott International also had a clear business
agenda that addressed a social need. Over two-thirds of
the company's 131,000 employees are entry level, lower-
wage workers in housekeeping, engineering, security,
maintenance, food service, and reservations. Developing
an effective method to recruit, train, and retain workers
in these positions has always been a critical concern.
Throughout the 1980s, Marriott had reached out to
untapped pockets of the labor market, such as Vietnam

veterans, ex-offenders, the disabled, recent immigrants, and welfare mothers. Although the company received tax credits as a financial incentive, Marriott continued to be plagued by a high level of turnover and poor job performance. By the beginning of the 1990s, the company badly needed new sources of reliable labor. After some experimentation, the first viable Pathways program was launched in Atlanta, Georgia, in 1991. Since then, Marriott has not only reduced turnover rates but also improved job prospects in inner cities.

STRONG PARTNERS COMMITTED TO CHANGE

A critical feature of the new paradigm is the presence of committed social sector organizations and leaders who are already working on change. These can include public servants and community figures such as mayors, governors, school superintendents, and civic activists. Companies need such partners to bring together diverse constituencies and to provide political legitimacy. Strong support helps ensure that new solutions will create systemic change, not languish in isolated projects. Committed social partners can also help businesses win access to underserved markets—for example, the inner city—and they can build widespread support for other new ventures.

Consider how IBM chose partners for its Reinventing Education initiative. The company singled out school districts where leaders were thinking in new and creative ways. When evaluating grant proposals, IBM looked for widely communicated education reform goals and strategic plans that clearly identified where projects could add value. The backing of strong mayors who were personally committed to education reform was considered vital. Mayor Edward Rendell, for example, supported superintendent David Hornbeck's program, Children Achieving in Philadelphia. The program showed how business involvement could contribute and was a major factor behind IBM's decision to invest there. Similarly, in Florida, Broward County's nine-point vision statement and five-year information technology plan were crucial in convincing IBM to get involved. By seizing on local agendas, IBM ensured that its projects would command the personal attention of superintendents and other key figures.

Bell Atlantic also found willing partners already working on major change. A key factor in getting Project Explore started was the commitment of Thomas Highton, superintendent of schools, and Congressman Robert Menendez, then state senator and mayor of Union City. When Highton was promoted to superintendent in 1988, Union City schools were failing on almost all scores. There was very little teacher involvement in decision making or parent involvement in their children's education; facilities were in poor shape; the curriculum was outdated; there was little to no technology. Highton proposed to turn an abandoned parochial school into a technology school, an action that required state approval. For his part, Menendez wanted to get fiber-optic networks throughout New Jersey to improve education and health services. Bell Atlantic's proposal was timely. The company's commitment to Union City, brokered by Menendez, gave Highton the credibility he needed to get approval to buy the abandoned parochial school. The school was renamed after Christopher Columbus to reflect the journey of discovery ahead in the trial called Project Explore.

Partners for educational projects are easily identifiable because schools are large and highly organized.

Companies confronting other social needs, however, may encounter many small nonprofit organizations, each of which works on a different piece of the problem. Marriott worked with various government and nonprofit partners in each of its Pathways to Independence programs—organizations such as Goodwill Industries, the Jewish Vocational Service, Private Industry Councils, and Workforce Development Boards. Marriott chose the strongest partner in each community.

The best way to ensure full commitment is to have both partners put their resources on the line.

United Airlines was also confronted with a patchwork of small community organizations working with welfare recipients. In launching its welfare-to-work efforts in San Francisco, United chose one strong nonprofit placement organization to be its lead partner and urged other groups to work through that agency. The details differ, but in all cases, strong partnerships are a crucial aspect of the new paradigm.

INVESTMENT BY BOTH PARTIES

The best way to ensure full commitment is to have both partners—not just the corporate but the community partner—put their resources on the line. Investment by both partners builds mutuality. It also ensures that the community partner will sustain the activities when contributions from business taper off.

In all of IBM's Reinventing Education initiatives, both partners put their hands in their pockets. IBM gave each school system a $2 million grant—up to 25% in cash and 75% or more in technical equipment, software, research, and consulting time. The team at each site determined the mix. Almost all of IBM's grant to Broward County, for example, went toward consulting time.

The schools also contributed financially to the projects, both in the development phase and when full roll-out took place after the money ran out. The Philadelphia school system, for example, bought at least 109 computers in addition to the 36 PCs and 8 ThinkPads provided by IBM. Individual school principals also supplemented IBM and central office funds from their own budgets. To help manage the transition to internal leadership in Broward County, for instance, the schools paid for an IBM project manager and systems architect to remain for several months after grant funds were expended. Each school district also used considerable funds on staff time for planning and training, in addition to major technology investments.

BankBoston and its community partners sometimes share the costs of First Community Bank's projects. In Hartford, Connecticut, First Community Bank worked with the South Hartford Initiative, a community development organization, to establish a unique small-business lending program in 1997. That innovation took many months to structure and negotiate. First Community Bank funds an average of 46% of each loan in South Hartford Initiative's neighborhoods; SHI funds the balance on a fully subordinated basis. First Community Bank reduces its normal commitment fee and interest rate, and SHI agrees to collect only interest for the term of the loan, until the principal amount is due. SHI has the option to underwrite loans declined by the bank, and First Community then services those loans.

Investment by both parties means more than just financial investments. Consider the Pathways to Independence program. Some of Marriott's partners make

IBM does not rely on volunteers or part-time staff. It recruits the best talent it can for assignments.

direct financial contributions: Goodwill Industries reimburses over half of the program's costs of approximately $5,000 per student in those cities in which it is Marriott's partner. But even partners that don't contribute financially commit resources. For example, while Marriott provides uniforms, lunches, training sites, program management, on-the-job training, and mentoring, its partners help locate and screen candidates and assist them with housing, child care, and transportation.

During the life of an innovation project, the balance of investments can shift. Bell Atlantic bore the bulk of the costs for Project Explore when it was launched in 1993, after two years of planning. The company wired the new Columbus Middle School; trained the teachers; and gave 135 seventh graders and their teachers computers in their homes, along with printers and access to the Internet. Once involved, Bell Atlantic found its commitment growing. Even when the project had moved beyond a trial phase and had to compete for company resources every year, Bell Atlantic kept a project team on board to follow the group through seventh and eighth grades and into Emerson High. By 1995, Union City began to pick up the bills. The school system received a National Science Foundation grant to wire Emerson High School and buy most of the computers. By 1997, Union City was picking up 100% of the cost, although a part-time project manager from Bell Atlantic's Opportunity New Jersey remained to maintain the relationship.

Both partners also need to make strong staff commitments. IBM ensures that responsibilities in this area are balanced: a school-district project sponsor is matched with an IBM project executive, and a school district project manager with an IBM on-site project manager. IBM does not rely on volunteers or part-time staff. It recruits the best talent it can for assignments, which are considered challenging as well as personally rewarding. Participants in the programs must report their monthly costs and expenses—just as they would report them to the CEO of a client company. Says an IBM official, "We treat our school partners the way we treat our best customers."

The experience of working so closely with businesses has had a deep impact on organizations in the social sector. Schools involved in the Bell Atlantic and IBM experiments, for example, have found that they have had to become more efficient and market-oriented in selecting staff for the projects.

ROOTEDNESS IN THE USER COMMUNITY

Innovation is facilitated when developers learn directly from user experience. Therefore, IBM's projects were designed to bring technologists close to the schools. In Broward County, the initial IBM office was housed in the computer lab at Sunrise Middle School. This location enabled constant interaction between IBM staff and teachers who evaluated the software. Moreover, becoming part of the school environment fostered rapid acceptance of the IBM team. "They even ate cafeteria food," an administrator exclaimed.

Yet even when a company goes on-site, there can be cultural obstacles. IBM employees tended to see school procedures as bureaucratic, while teachers had negative stereotypes of people working in large corporations. "We move at different speeds," one IBM team member explained. Cultural differences were also apparent in language—jargon was a significant barrier to communication. According to one IBM employee, the "educational world has even more acronyms than the IBM world, which surprised everybody." But over time, the presence of IBM people in the schools, and their openness to learn from educators, helped bridge the differences and allayed many of the schools' concerns that they would be taken over by businesspeople.

In the inner-city neighborhoods in which it operates, BankBoston's First Community Bank takes great care in staffing its branches to ensure that the employees understand the community. First Community Bank founder and president Gail Snowden, for example, grew up in the bank's core neighborhood, where her parents ran a well-regarded community service organization. First Community Bank managers are expected to attend community events as part of their job. The bank has created new functions—such as community development officers who act as liaisons with customers in specific ethnic populations—to further embed it in its communities. The bank also offers customized technical assistance—for example, document translation or explanation of customs to new immigrants. Although these service innovations increase the time spent per transaction, they make First Community Bank branches part of the fabric of the neighborhood. That helps make parent BankBoston a leader in the urban market.

LINKS TO OTHER ORGANIZATIONS

For projects to succeed, the business partner must call on the expertise of key players in the broader community. Bell Atlantic, for example, brought in the Stevens Institute of Technology—which had expertise in Internet capabilities and equipment configurations—to help build a curriculum for teachers around Internet access. Similarly, IBM nurtured connections with the school districts' other partners, some of which already had a deep local presence. In Philadelphia, IBM relied on the Philadelphia Education Fund—an offshoot of Greater Philadelphia First, a coalition of the city's 35 largest corporations—as a source of local knowledge. In Cincinnati, IBM convened businesses and funders such as Procter & Gamble and General Electric to ensure that everyone worked toward the same ends in the schools.

BankBoston, too, finds its broader community and government contacts to be useful sources of additional ideas and finance for riskier deals and start-up businesses. First Community Bank's community development group, for instance, worked with about eight other banks and the U.S. Small Business Administration to create a new "fast track"

Test sites, by nature, receive concentrated attention. The real challenge is replicating the project elsewhere.

SBA loan approval. Without external collaboration, no business innovation partnership can expect to enact lasting change.

A LONG-TERM COMMITMENT TO SUSTAIN
AND REPLICATE THE SOLUTION

Like any R&D project, new-paradigm partnerships
require sustained commitment. The inherent uncertainty of innovation—trying something that has never
been done before in that particular setting—means that
initial project plans are best guesses, not firm forecasts.
Events beyond the company's control, unexpected obstacles in technology, political complexities, new opportunities or technologies unknown at the time plans were
made—all of these can derail the best-laid plans. First
Community Bank took five years to show a profit, but
last year it was number one in sales out of all of Bank-
Boston's retail operations. Investments in the social sector, just as in any start-up, require patient capital.

Each of the new-paradigm companies described
wanted to create a successful prototype or demonstration project in the test site. But test sites, by nature,
receive concentrated attention and resources. The real
challenge is not sustaining an individual project but
replicating it elsewhere. The best innovations can be
mass-produced, adopted by users in other settings, and
supported by additional investors. That is why replica-
tion and extension were explicit parts of IBM's strategy.

The Reinventing Education project began in ten
school districts. First-round grants from IBM covered a
three- to five-year period, and IBM wanted most of the
money disbursed in the first two years so that the next
three could be spent diffusing the innovation and examining the project's impact. Tools developed in the first
round of innovations were then introduced through an
additional 12 projects. To help the sites complete their
individual rollouts, IBM staff continue to monitor sites

for five years. IBM encourages cross-fertilization of ideas among all the Reinventing Education project sites. Broward County, for example, hosts officials from other school districts on a quarterly basis. Charlotte-Mecklenburg's Wired for Learning prototype is spreading throughout North Carolina. And an IBM Web site discussion forum also helps spread ideas among the project sites—an arrangement that is beneficial both to schools and to IBM.

How Business Benefits

Sometimes business attempts to find innovation in the social sector are discounted by critics as public relations ploys. But as the depth and breadth of each company's commitment should make clear, that would be an extremely costly and risky way to get favorable press. The extensive efforts described here, with their goal of creating systemic change, also cannot be justified only on the grounds that they make employees or the community feel good—even though that obviously motivates people to work hard. In reality, the primary business justification for the sustained commitment of resources is the new knowledge and capabilities that will stem from innovation—the lessons learned from the tough problems solved.

Bell Atlantic's Project Explore was expensive, and it was not philanthropy. It was funded out of operating and technology-development budgets. Certainly, Bell Atlantic people felt good about helping inner-city schoolchildren succeed. And the company generates a continuing and growing revenue stream from selling network services to the education market, which it learned how to approach from its extensive experience in Union City. But the ultimate business justification for Project Explore was the know-how Bell Atlantic developed about networking technologies. As John Grady, now HDSL product manager but then the first Union City project manager, puts it, "the Union City trial provided the first evidence that HDSL technology could work." In April 1997, Grady and three other Bell Atlantic employees received a patent for a public-switch telephone network for multimedia transmission—a direct consequence of the innovations developed in Union City. That patent ultimately led to the introduction of Bell Atlantic's new Infospeed DSL product line in 1999.

IBM, too, stretches its technical capabilities by tackling the difficult problems in public schools. IBM employees experimented with new technology that has commercial applications. For the Reinventing Education project in Cincinnati, for example, IBM researchers developed new drag-and-drop technology for the Internet, which uses the latest features of Java and HTML and can be leveraged throughout IBM. As a systems architect in Cincinnati remarked, "The group that I'm working with and I have learned more on this project than any other that we've worked on previously. We're working with people from the ground up. When we started, there was absolutely nothing except an idea about new Internet technology." And the Broward County project extended IBM's data-warehousing know-how from small groups of users in retailing and related industries to very large groups of users with complicated

It cost Marriott $2 million to set up the hot line; it now saves $4 for every dollar spent, through lower turnover and reduced absenteeism.

data requirements—over 10,000 teachers and administrators in a school system.

Marriott's Pathways to Independence has produced
tangible benefits for the company. About 70% of Pathways' graduates are still employed by Marriott after a
year, compared with only 45% of the welfare hires who
did not participate in Pathways and only 50% of other
new hires. Marriott estimates that program costs are
recovered if graduates are retained 2.5 times longer than
the average new hire. In fact, Pathways is considered to
be such a source of competitive advantage for Marriott
that the company shares only the general outlines of the
program with other companies and keeps the details
proprietary. And success in the Pathways to Independence program has encouraged Marriott to undertake
other initiatives, such as the Associate Resource Line, a
hot line that provides assistance with housing, transportation, immigration, financial and legal issues, even
pet care. It cost Marriott $2 million to set up the hot line;
it now saves $4 for every dollar spent, through lower
turnover and reduced absenteeism.

BankBoston, too, has found business benefits from its
social initiative. Its First Community Bank has become
both a profitable operating unit and a source of product
and service innovations that have been applied across all
of BankBoston. These include First Step products for
newcomers to banking; multilingual ATMs; a new
venture-capital unit for equity investments in inner-
city businesses; and community development officers,
who help create lending opportunities. In fact, First Community bank has been so successful that BankBoston is
refocusing its retail strategy toward community banking.

Employees' opinions of the initiative have also been
transformed. Far from being a dead-end assignment, a

position at First Community Bank is highly desirable because it offers the challenge and excitement of innovation. In January 1999, founding president Gail Snowden was promoted to head up the regional leadership group for all of BankBoston's retail banking. And in March 1999, President Clinton presented BankBoston with the Ron Brown Award for Corporate Leadership (for which I was a judge) in recognition of its community-banking activities. Clearly, businesses that partake in these new-paradigm partnerships reap tangible benefits.

Spreading the New Paradigm

This article describes a new way for companies to approach the social sector: not as an object of charity but as an opportunity for learning and business development, supported by R&D and operating funds rather than philanthropy. Traditional charity and volunteerism have an important role in society, but they are often not the best or fastest way to produce innovation or transformation.

High-impact business contributions to the social sector use the core competencies of a business—the things it does best. For Bell Atlantic, it is communications technology; for IBM, it is information technology solutions; for Marriott, it is service strategies. In this new paradigm, the activities are focused on results, seeking measurable outcomes and demonstrated changes. The effort can be sustained and replicated in other places. The community gets new approaches that build capabilities and point the way to permanent improvements. The business gets bottom-line benefits: new products, new solutions to critical problems, and new market opportunities.

New-paradigm partnerships could reinvent American institutions. They open new possibilities for solving recalcitrant social and educational problems. They give businesses a new way to innovate. Today these examples are still works in progress. But tomorrow they could be the way business is done everywhere.

Why America Needs Corporate Social Innovation

DESPITE ITS LONG ECONOMIC BOOM, America's social problems abound. To ensure future economic success, the country needs dramatic improvement in public schools, more highly skilled workers, jobs with a future for people coming off the welfare rolls, revitalized urban centers and inner cities, and healthy communities. Traditionally, businesses have supported the social sector in two different ways: they contribute their employees' time for volunteer activities, and they support community initiatives with money and gifts in kind. Both activities can accomplish many good things and should be encouraged, but neither activity engages the unique skills and capabilities of business.

Consider the typical corporate volunteer program. It almost invariably draws on the lowest common skills in a company by mobilizing people to do physical work—landscaping a school's grounds or painting walls in a community center. Such projects are good for team building and may augment limited community budgets, even build new relationships, but they don't change the education system or strengthen economic prospects for community residents. In many cases, it is just as effective for the business simply to write a check to community residents or a small neighborhood organization to do the work.

And that, indeed, is what many companies do. A great deal of business participation in social sector problems derives from the classic model of arm's-length charity—writing a check and leaving everything else to government and nonprofit agencies. Businesses have little involvement in how these donations are used. In fact, this model actively discourages companies from taking an interest in results. Companies receive their benefits upfront through tax write-offs and the public relations boost that accompanies the announcement of their largesse. There is little or no incentive to stay involved or to take responsibility for seeing that the contribution is used to reach a goal. However well meaning, many businesses treat the social sector as a charity case—a dumping ground for spare cash, obsolete equipment, and tired executives on their way out.

Such arm's-length models of corporate philanthropy have not produced fundamental solutions to America's most urgent domestic problems of public education, jobs for the disadvantaged, and neighborhood revitalization. Nor will they, because traditional charity can't reach the root of the problems; it just treats the symptoms. Most business partnerships with schools, for example, are limited in scope: they usually provide local resources to augment a school program, such as scholarship funds, career days, sponsorship of an athletic team, or volunteer reading tutors. The criteria for involvement are minimal, often hinging only on geographic proximity to a company site. The 600 school principals I surveyed said they are grateful for any help from the business sector. But what they really want today, when public education is under attack, are new ideas for systemic change that private enterprises are uniquely qualified to contribute.

As government downsizes and the public expects the private sector to step in to help solve community problems, it is important that businesses understand why the old models of corporate support don't create sustainable change. In partnership with government and nonprofits, businesses need to go beyond the traditional models to tackle the much tougher task of innovation.

Originally published in May–June 1999
Reprint 99306

Enlightened Experimentation

The New Imperative for Innovation

STEFAN THOMKE

Executive Summary

THE HIGH COST OF EXPERIMENTATION has long put a damper on companies' attempts to create great new products. But new technologies are making it easier than ever to conduct complex experiments quickly and cheaply. Companies can now take innovation to a whole new level, contends Stefan Thomke, if they're willing to rethink their R&D from the ground up.

Understanding what enlightened experimentation is all about requires an appreciation of the innovation process. All development organizations need a *system* of experimentation in place to help them decide which ideas to pursue. Of course, the more rapid and efficient the system is, the quicker researchers can find solutions. Many companies today, however, mistakenly view technologies solely in terms of cost cutting. They overlook the fact that some technologies can introduce entirely new ways of discovering novel concepts and solutions.

Thomke argues that new technologies affect everything, from the development process itself—including the way an R&D organization is structured—to how new knowledge is created. So companies that are trying to be more innovative face both managerial and technical challenges. Drawing on his research in the pharmaceutical, automotive, and software industries, Thomke introduces the following four rules for enlightened experimentation: organize for rapid experimentation; fail early and often, but avoid mistakes; anticipate and exploit early information; and combine new and old technologies.

The article users real-world examples to explain each rule in detail. It also suggests how this system of experimentation will affect other industries and examines the implications for knowledge workers.

EXPERIMENTATION LIES at the heart of every company's ability to innovate. In other words, the systematic testing of ideas is what enables companies to create and refine their products. In fact, no product can be a product without having first been an idea that was shaped, to one degree or another, through the process of experimentation. Today, a major development project can require literally thousands of experiments, all with the same objective: to learn whether the product concept or proposed technical solution holds promise for addressing a new need or problem, then incorporating that information in the next round of tests so that the best product ultimately results.

In the past, testing was relatively expensive, so companies had to be parsimonious with the number of experimental iterations. Today, however, new technologies such as computer simulation, rapid prototyping, and combinatorial chemistry allow companies to create more learning more rapidly, and that knowledge, in turn, can be incorporated in more experiments at less expense. Indeed, new information-based technologies have driven down the marginal costs of experimentation, just as they have decreased the marginal costs in some production and distribution systems. Moreover, an experimental system that integrates new information-based technologies does more than lower costs; it also increases the opportunities for innovation. That is, some technologies can make existing experimental activities more efficient, while others introduce entirely new ways of discovering novel concepts and solutions.

Millennium Pharmaceuticals in Cambridge, Massachusetts, for instance, incorporates new technologies such as genomics, bioinformatics, and combinatorial chemistry in its technology platform for conducting experiments. The platform enables factory-like automation that can generate and test drug candidates in minutes or seconds, compared with the days or more that traditional methods require. Gaining information early on about, say, the toxicological profile of a drug candidate significantly improves Millennium's ability to predict the drug's success in clinical testing and, ultimately, in the marketplace. Unpromising candidates are eliminated before hundreds of millions of dollars are invested in their development. In addition to reducing the cost and time of traditional drug development, the new technologies also enhance Millennium's ability to innovate, according to Chief Technology Officer Michael Pavia. Specifically, the company has greater opportunities to experiment with more diverse potential drugs, including those that may initially seem improbable but might eventually lead to breakthrough discoveries.

This era of "enlightened experimentation" has thus far affected businesses with high costs of product development, such as the pharmaceutical, automotive, and software industries. By studying them, I have learned several valuable lessons that I believe have broad applicability to other industries. As the cost of computing continues to fall, making all sorts of complex calculations faster and cheaper, and as new technologies like combinatorial chemistry emerge, virtually all companies will discover that they have a greater capacity for rapid experimentation to investigate diverse concepts. Financial institutions, for example, now use computer simulations to test new financial instruments. In fact, the development of spreadsheet software has forever changed financial modeling; even novices can perform many sophisticated what-if experiments that were once prohibitively expensive.

A System for Experimentation

Understanding enlightened experimentation requires an appreciation of the process of innovation. Namely, product and technology innovations don't drop from the sky; they are nurtured in laboratories and development organizations, passing through a *system* for experimentation. All development organizations have such a system in place to help them narrow the number of ideas to pursue and then refine that group into what can become viable products. A critical stage of the process occurs when an idea or concept becomes a working artifact, or prototype, which can then be tested, discussed, shown to customers, and learned from.

Perhaps the most famous example of the experimental system at work comes from the laboratories of Thomas Alva Edison. When Edison noted that inventive genius is "99% perspiration and 1% inspiration," he was well aware of the importance of an organization's capability and capacity to experiment. That's why he designed his operations in Menlo Park, New Jersey, to allow for efficient and rapid experimental iterations.

Edison knew that the various components of a system for experimentation—including personnel, equipment, libraries, and so on—all function interdependently. As such, they need to be jointly optimized, for together they define the system's performance: its speed (the time needed to design, build, test, and analyze an experiment), cost, fidelity (the accuracy of the experiment and the conditions under which it is conducted), capacity (the number of experiments that can be performed in a given time period), and the learning gained (the amount of new information generated by the experiment and an organization's ability to benefit from it). Thus, for example, highly skilled machinists worked in close proximity to lab personnel at Menlo Park so they could quickly make improvements when researchers had new ideas or learned something new from previous experiments. This system led to landmark inventions, including the electric lightbulb, which required more than 1,000 complex experiments with filament materials and shapes, electromechanical regulators, and vacuum technologies.

Edison's objective of achieving great innovation through rapid and frequent experimentation is especially pertinent today as the costs (both financial and time) of experimentation plunge. Yet many companies mistakenly view new technologies solely in terms of cost cutting, overlooking their vast potential for innovation. Worse, companies with that limited view get bogged down in the confusion that occurs when they try to incorporate new technologies. For instance, computer simulation doesn't simply replace physical prototypes as a cost-saving measure; it introduces an entirely different way of experimenting that invites innovation. Just as the Internet offers enormous opportunities for innovation—far surpassing its use as a low-cost substitute for phone or catalog transactions—so does state-of-the-art experimentation. But realizing that potential requires companies to adopt a different mind-set.

Indeed, new technologies affect everything, from the development process itself, including the way an R&D organization is structured, to how new knowledge—and hence learning—is created. Thus, for companies to be more innovative, the challenges are managerial as well as technical, as these four rules for enlightened experimentation suggest:

1. ORGANIZE FOR RAPID EXPERIMENTATION

The ability to experiment quickly is integral to innovation: as developers conceive of a multitude of diverse ideas, experiments can provide the rapid feedback necessary to shape those ideas by reinforcing, modifying, or complementing existing knowledge. Rapid experimentation, however, often requires the complete revamping of entrenched routines. When, for example, certain classes of experiments become an order of magnitude cheaper or faster, organizational incentives may suddenly become misaligned, and the activities and routines that were once successful might become hindrances. (See "The Potential Pitfalls of New Technologies" at the end of this article.)

Consider the major changes that BMW recently underwent. Only a few years ago, experimenting with novel design concepts—to make cars withstand crashes better, for instance—required expensive physical prototypes to be built. Because that process took months, it acted as a barrier to innovation because engineers could not get timely feedback on their ideas. Furthermore, data from crash tests arrived too late to significantly influence decisions in the early stages of product development. So BMW had to incorporate the information far downstream, incurring greater costs. Nevertheless, BMW's R&D organization, structured around this traditional system, developed award-winning automobiles, cementing the company's reputation as an industry leader. But its success also made change difficult.

Today, thanks to virtual experiments—crashes simulated by a high-performance computer rather than through physical prototypes—some of the information arrives very early, before BMW has made major resource decisions. The costs of experimentation (both financial and time) are therefore lower because BMW eliminates the creation of physical prototypes as well as the expense of potentially reworking bad designs after the company has committed itself to them. (Physical prototypes are still required much further downstream to verify the final designs and meet safety regulations.) In addition, the rapid feedback and the ability to see and manipulate high-quality computer images spur greater innovation: many design possibilities can be explored in "real time" yet virtually, in rapid iterations.

To study this new technology's impact on innovation, BMW performed the following experiment. Several designers, a simulation engineer, and a test engineer formed a team to improve the side-impact safety of cars. Primarily using computer simulations, the team developed and tested new ideas that resulted from their frequent brainstorming meetings.

Because all the knowledge required about safety, design, simulation, and testing resided within a small group, the team was able to iterate experiments and develop solutions rapidly. After each round of simulated crashes, the team analyzed the results and developed new ideas for the next round of experiments. As expected, the team benefited greatly from the rapid feedback: it took them only a few days to accept, refine, or reject new design solutions—something that had once taken months.

As the trials accrued, the group members greatly increased their knowledge of the underlying mechanics, which enabled them to design previously unimaginable experiments. In fact, one test completely changed their knowledge about the complex relationship between material strength and safety. Specifically, BMW's engineers had assumed that the stronger the area next to the bottom of a car's pillars (the structures that connect the roof of an auto to its chassis), the better the vehicle would be able to withstand crashes. But one member of the development team insisted on verifying this assumption through an inexpensive computer simulation.

The results shocked the team: strengthening a particular area below one of the pillars substantially *decreased* the vehicle's crashworthiness. After more experiments and careful analysis, the engineers discovered that strengthening the lower part of the center pillar would make the pillar prone to folding higher up, above the strengthened area. Thus, the passenger compartment would be more penetrable at the part of the car closer to the midsection, chest, and head of passengers. The solution was to weaken, not strengthen, the lower area. This counterintuitive knowledge—that purposely weakening a part of a car's structure could increase the vehicle's safety—has led BMW to reevaluate all the reinforced areas of its vehicles.

In summary, this small team increased the side-impact crash safety by about 30%. It is worth noting that two crash tests of physical prototypes at the end of the project confirmed the simulation results. It should also be noted that the physical prototypes cost a total of about $300,000, which was more than the cost of all 91 virtual crashes combined. Furthermore, the physical prototypes took longer to build, prepare, and test than the entire series of virtual crashes.

But to obtain the full benefits of simulation technologies, BMW had to undertake sweeping changes in process, organization, and attitude—changes that took several years to accomplish. Not only did the company have to reorganize the way different groups worked together; it also had to change habits that had worked so well in the old sequential development process.

Previously, for example, engineers were often loath to release less-than-perfect data. To some extent, it was in each group's interest to hold back and monitor the output from other groups. After all, the group that submitted its information to a central database first would quite likely have to make the most changes because it would have gotten the least feedback from other areas. So, for instance, the door development team at BMW was accustomed to—and rewarded for—releasing nearly flawless data (details about the material strength of a proposed door, for example), which could take many months to generate. The idea of releasing rough information very early, an integral part of a rapid and parallel experimentation process, was unthinkable—and not built into the incentive system. Yet a six-month delay while data were being perfected could derail a development program predicated on rapid iterations.

Thus, to encourage the early sharing of information, BMW's managers had to ensure that each group understood and appreciated the needs of other teams. The crash simulation group, for example, needed to make the door designers aware of the information it required in order to build rough models for early-stage crash simulations. That transfer of knowledge had a ripple effect, changing how the door designers worked because some of the requested information demanded that they pay close attention to the needs of other groups as well. They started to understand that withholding information as long as possible was counterproductive. By making these kinds of organizational changes, BMW in Germany significantly slashed development time and costs and boosted innovation.

2. FAIL EARLY AND OFTEN, BUT AVOID MISTAKES

Experimenting with many diverse—and sometimes seemingly absurd—ideas is crucial to innovation. When a novel concept fails in an experiment, the failure can expose important gaps in knowledge. Such experiments are particularly desirable when they are performed early on so that unfavorable options can be eliminated quickly and people can refocus their efforts on more promising alternatives. Building the capacity for rapid experimentation in early development means rethinking the role of failure in organizations. Positive failure requires having a thick skin, says David Kelley, founder of IDEO, a leading design firm in Palo Alto, California.

IDEO encourages its designers "to fail often to succeed sooner," and the company understands that more radical experiments frequently lead to more spectacular failures. Indeed, IDEO has developed numerous prototypes that have bordered on the ridiculous (and were later rejected), such as shoes with toy figurines on the shoelaces. At the same time, IDEO's approach has led to a host of best-sellers, such as the Palm V handheld computer, which has made the company the subject of intense media interest, including a *Nightline* segment with Ted Koppel and coverage in *Serious Play*, a book by Michael Schrage, a codirector of the e-markets initiative at the MIT Media Lab, that describes the crucial importance of allowing innovators to play with prototypes.

Removing the stigma of failure, though, usually requires overcoming ingrained attitudes. People who fail in experiments are often viewed as incompetent, and that attitude can lead to counterproductive behavior. As Kelley points out, developers who are afraid of failing and looking bad to management will sometimes build expensive, sleek prototypes that they become committed to before they know any of the answers. In other words, the sleek prototype might look impressive, but it presents the false impression that the product is farther along than it really is, and that perception subtly discourages people from changing the design even though better alternatives might exist. That's why IDEO advocates the development of cheap, rough prototypes that people are invited to criticize—a process that eventually leads to better products. "You have to have the guts to create a straw man," asserts Kelley.

To foster a culture in which people aren't afraid of failing, IDEO has created a playroomlike atmosphere. On Mondays, the different branches hold show-and-tells in which employees display and talk about their latest ideas and products. IDEO also maintains a giant "tech box" of hundreds of gadgets and curiosities that designers routinely rummage through, seeking inspiration among the switches, buttons, and various odd materials and objects. And brainstorming sessions, in which wild ideas are encouraged and participants defer judgment to avoid damping the discussion, are a staple of the different project groups.

3M is another company with a healthy attitude toward failure. 3M's product groups often have skunkworks teams that investigate the opportunities (or difficulties) that a potential product might pose. The teams, consisting primarily of technical people, including manufacturing engineers, face little repercussion if an idea flops—indeed, sometimes a failure is cause for celebration. When a team discovers that a potential product doesn't work, the group quickly disbands and its members move on to other projects.

Failures, however, should not be confused with mistakes. Mistakes produce little new or useful information and are therefore without value. A poorly planned or badly conducted experiment, for instance, might result in ambiguous data, forcing researchers to repeat the experiment. Another common mistake is repeating a prior failure or being unable to learn from that experience. Unfortunately, even the best organizations often lack the management systems necessary to carefully distinguish between failures and mistakes.

3. ANTICIPATE AND EXPLOIT EARLY INFORMATION

When important projects fail late in the game, the consequences can be devastating. In the pharmaceutical industry, for example, more than 80% of drug candidates are discontinued during the clinical development phases, where more than half of total project expenses can be incurred. Yet although companies are often forced to spend millions of dollars to correct problems in the later stages of product development, they generally underestimate the cost savings of early problem solving. Studies of software development, for instance, have shown that late-stage problems are more than 100 times as costly as early-stage ones. For other environments that involve large capital investments in production equipment, the increase in cost can be orders of magnitude higher.

In addition to financial costs, companies need to consider the value of time when those late-stage problems are on a project's critical path—as they often are. In pharmaceuticals, shaving six months off drug development means effectively extending patent protection when the product hits the market. Similarly, an electronics company might easily find that six months account for a quarter of a product's life cycle and a third of all profits.

New technologies, then, can provide some of their greatest leverage by identifying and solving problems upstream—best described as *front-loaded development*.

In the automotive industry, for example, "quick-and-dirty" crash simulations on a computer can help companies avoid potential safety problems downstream. Such simulations may not be as complete or as perfect as late-stage prototypes will be, but they can force organizational problem solving and communication at a time when many downstream groups are not participating directly in development. (See "The Benefits of Front-Loaded Development" at the end of this article.)

Several years ago, Chrysler (now DaimlerChrysler) discovered the power of three-dimensional computer models, known internally as digital mock-ups, for identifying certain problems in early development stages. When Chrysler developed the 1993 Concorde and Dodge Intrepid models, the process of decking—placing the power train and related components like the exhaust and suspension in the prototype automobile—took more than three weeks and required many attempts before the powertrain could be inserted successfully. By contrast, the early use of digital mock-ups in the 1998 Concorde and Intrepid models allowed the company to simulate decking to identify (and solve) numerous interference problems before the physical decking took place. Instead of taking weeks, decking was completed in 15 minutes because all obstruction problems had been resolved earlier—when it was relatively inexpensive and fast to do so.

Of course, it is neither pragmatic nor economically feasible for companies to obtain all the early information they would like. So IDEO follows the principle of three R's: rough, rapid, and right. The final R recognizes that early prototypes may be incomplete but can still get specific aspects of a product right. For example, to design a telephone receiver, an IDEO team carved dozens of pieces of foam and cradled them between their heads and shoulders to find the best possible shape for a handset. While incomplete as a telephone, the model focused on getting 100% of the shape right. Perhaps the main advantage of this approach is that it forces people to decide judiciously which factors can initially be rough and which must be right. With its three R's, IDEO has established a process that generates important information when it is most valuable: the early stages of development.

In addition to saving time and money, exploiting early information helps product developers keep up with customer preferences that might evolve over the course of a project. As many companies can attest, customers will often say about a finished product: "This is exactly what I asked you to develop, but it is not what I want." Leading software businesses typically show incomplete prototypes to customers in so-called beta tests, and through that process they often discover changes and problems when they are still fairly inexpensive to handle.

4. COMBINE NEW AND TRADITIONAL TECHNOLOGIES

New technologies that are used in the innovation process itself are designed to help solve problems as part of an experimentation *system*. A company must therefore understand how to use and manage new and traditional technologies together so that they complement each other. In fact, research by Marco Iansiti of Harvard Business School has found that, in many industries, the ability to integrate technologies is crucial to developing superior products.

A new technology often reaches the same general performance of its traditional counterpart much more quickly and at a lower cost. But the new technology usually performs at only 70% to 80% of the established technology. For example, a new chemical synthesis process might be able to obtain a purity level that is just three-quarters that of a mature technique. Thus, by combining new and established technologies, organizations can avoid the performance gap while also enjoying the benefits of cheaper and faster experimentation. (See the exhibit "Combining the New with the Traditional.")

Indeed, the true potential of new technologies lies in a company's ability to reconfigure its processes and organization to use them in concert with traditional technologies. Eventually, a new technology can replace its traditional counterpart, but it then might be challenged by a newer technology that must be integrated. To understand this complex evolution, consider what has happened in the pharmaceutical industry.

In the late nineteenth century and for much of the twentieth century, drug development occurred through a process of systematic trial-and-error experiments. Scientists would start with little or no knowledge about a particular disease and try out numerous molecules, many from their company's chemical libraries, until they found one that happened to work. Drugs can be likened to keys that need to fit the locks of targets, such as the specific nerve cell receptors associated with central nervous diseases. Metaphorically, then, chemists were once blind, or at least semiblind, locksmiths who have had to make up thousands of different keys to find the one that matched. Doing so entailed synthesizing compounds, one at a time, each of which usually required several days at a cost from \$5,000 to \$10,000.

Typically, for each successful drug that makes it to market, a company investigates roughly 10,000 starting candidates. Of those, only 1,000 compounds make it to more extensive trials in vitro (that is, outside living organisms in settings such as test tubes), 20 of which are tested even more extensively in vivo (that is, in the body of a living organism such as a mouse), and ten of which

---

Combining the New with the Traditional

A new technology will reach perhaps just 70% to 80% of the performance of an established technology. A new computer model, for instance, might be able to represent real-world functionality that is just three-quarters that of an advanced prototype model. To avoid this performance gap—and potentially create new opportunities for innovation—companies can use the new and traditional technologies in concert. The optimal time for switching between the two occurs when the rates of improvement between the new and mature technologies are about the same—that is, when the slopes of the two curves are equal.

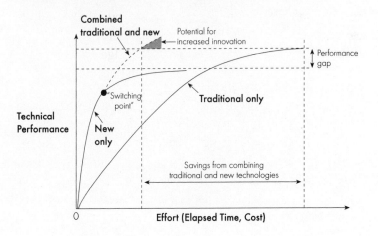

make it to clinical trials with humans. The entire process represents a long and costly commitment.

But in the last ten years, new technologies have significantly increased the efficiency and speed at which companies can generate and screen chemical compounds. Researchers no longer need to painstakingly create one compound at a time. Instead, they can use combinatorial chemistry, quickly generating numerous variations simultaneously around a few building blocks, just as today's locksmiths can make thousands of keys from a dozen basic shapes, thereby reducing the cost of a compound from thousands of dollars to a few dollars or less.

In practice, however, combinatorial chemistry has disrupted well-established routines in laboratories. For one thing, the rapid synthesis of drugs has led to a new problem: how to screen those compounds quickly. Traditionally, potential drugs were tested in live animals—an activity fraught with logistical difficulties, high expense, and considerable statistical variation.

So laboratories developed test-tube-based screening methodologies that could be automated. Called high-throughput screening, this technology requires significant innovations in equipment (such as high-speed precision robotics) and in the screening process itself to let researchers conduct a series of biological tests, or assays, on members of a chemical library virtually simultaneously.

The large pharmaceutical corporations and academic chemistry departments initially greeted such "combichem" technologies (combinatorial chemistry and high-throughput screening) with skepticism. Among the reasons cited was that the purity of compounds generated via combichem was relatively poor compared to traditional synthetic chemistry. As a result, many advances in the technology were made by small biotechnology companies.

But as the technology matured, it caught the interest of large corporations like Eli Lilly, which in 1994 acquired Sphinx Pharmaceuticals, one of the start-ups developing combichem. Eli Lilly took a few years to transfer the new technologies to its drug discovery division, which used traditional synthesis. To overcome the internal resistance, senior management implemented various mechanisms to control how the new technologies were being adopted. For example, it temporarily limited the in-house screening available to chemists, leaving them no choice but to use some of the high-throughput screening capabilities at the Sphinx subsidiary and interact with the staff there.

Until now, pharmaceutical giants like Eli Lilly have used combinatorial chemistry primarily to optimize promising new drug candidates that resulted from an exhaustive search through chemical libraries and other traditional sources. But as combinatorial chemistry itself advances and achieves levels of purity and diversity comparable to the compounds in a library, companies will increasingly use it at the earlier phases of drug discovery. In fact, all major pharmaceutical companies have had to use combichem and traditional synthesis in concert, and the companies that are best able to manage the new and mature technologies together so that they fully complement each other will have the greatest opportunity to achieve the highest gains in productivity and innovation.

Enlightened Implications

New technologies reduce the cost and time of experimentation, allowing companies to be more innovative. Automotive companies, for example, are currently advancing the performance of sophisticated safety systems that measure a passenger's position, weight, and height to adjust the force and speed at which airbags deploy. The availability of fast and inexpensive simulation enables the massive and rapid experimentation necessary to develop such complex safety devices.

But it is important to note that the increased automation of routine experiments will not remove the human element in innovation. On the contrary, it will allow people to focus on areas where their value is greatest: generating novel ideas and concepts, learning from experiments, and ultimately making decisions that require judgment. For example, although Millennium's R&D facilities look more and more like factories, the value of knowledge workers has actually increased. Instead of carrying out routine laboratory experiments, they now focus on the early stages (determining which experiments to conduct, for instance) and making sense of the information generated by the experimentation.

The implications for industries are enormous. The electronic spreadsheet has already revolutionized financial problem solving by driving down the marginal cost of financial experimentation to nearly zero; even a small start-up can perform complex cash-flow analyses on an inexpensive PC. Similarly, computer simulation and other technologies have enabled small businesses and individuals to rapidly experiment with novel designs of customized integrated circuits. The result has been a massive wave of innovation, ranging from smart toys to electronic devices. Previously, the high cost of integrated-circuit customization made such experimentation economical to only the largest companies.

Perhaps, though, this era of enlightened experimentation is still in its bare infancy. Indeed, the ultimate technology for rapid experimentation might turn out to be the Internet, which is already turning countless users into fervent innovators.

The Essentials for Enlightened Experimentation

NEW TECHNOLOGIES such as computer simulations not only make experimentation faster and cheaper, they also enable companies to be more innovative. But achieving that requires a thorough understanding of the link between experimentation and learning. Briefly stated, innovation requires the right R&D systems for performing experiments that will generate the information needed to develop and refine products quickly. The challenges are managerial as well as technical:

1) Organize for rapid experimentation

- Examine and, if necessary, revamp entrenched routines, organizational boundaries, and incentives to encourage rapid experimentation.

- Consider using small development groups that contain key people (designers, test engineers, manufacturing engineers) with all the knowledge required to iterate rapidly.

- Determine what experiments can be performed in parallel instead of sequentially. Parallel experiments are most effective when time matters most, cost is not an overriding factor, and developers expect to learn little that would guide them in planning the next round of experiments.

2) Fail early and often, but avoid mistakes

- Embrace failures that occur early in the development process and advance knowledge significantly.

- Don't forget the basics of experimentation. Well-designed tests have clear objectives (what do you anticipate learning?) and hypotheses (what do you expect to happen?). Also, mistakes often occur when you don't control variables that could diminish your ability to learn from the experiments. When variability can't be controlled, allow for multiple, repeated trials.

3) Anticipate and exploit early information

- Recognize the full value of front-loading: identifying problems upstream, where they are easier and cheaper to solve.

- Acknowledge the trade-off between cost and fidelity. Experiments of lower fidelity (generally costing less) are best suited in the early exploratory stages of developing a product. High-fidelity experiments (typically more expensive) are best suited later to verify the product.

4) Combine new and traditional technologies

- Do not assume that a new technology will necessarily replace an established one. Usually, new and traditional technologies are best used in concert.

- Remember that new technologies emerge and evolve continually. Today's new technology might eventually replace its traditional counterpart, but it could then be challenged by tomorrow's new technology.

The Potential Pitfalls of New Technologies

NEW TECHNOLOGIES can slash the costs (both financial and time) of experimentation and dramatically increase a company's ability to develop innovative products. To reap those benefits, though, organizations must prepare themselves for the full effects of such technologies.

Computer simulations and rapid prototyping, for example, increase not only a company's capacity to conduct experiments but also the wealth of information generated by those tests. That, however, can easily overload an organization that lacks the capability to process information from each round of experiments quickly enough to incorporate it into the next round. In such cases, the result is waste, confusion, and frustration. In other words, without careful and thorough planning, a new technology might not only fail to deliver on its promise of lower cost, increased speed, and greater innovation, it could actually decrease the overall performance of an R&D organization, or at a minimum disrupt its operations.

Misaligned objectives are another common problem. Specifically, some managers do not fully appreciate the trade-off between response time and resource utilization. Consider what happens when companies establish central departments to oversee computing resources for performing simulations. Clearly, testing ideas and concepts virtually can provide developers with the rapid feedback they need to shape new products. At the same time, computers are costly, so people managing them as cost centers are evaluated by how much those resources are being used.

The busier a central computer is, however, the longer it takes for developers to get the feedback they need. In fact, the relationship between waiting time and utilization is not linear—queuing theory has shown that the waiting time typically increases gradually until a resource is utilized around 70%, and then the length of the delays surge. (See the exhibit "Waiting for a Resource.") An organization trying to shave costs may become a victim of its own myopic objective. That is, an annual savings of perhaps a few hundred thousand dollars achieved through increasing utilization from 70% to 90% may lead to very long delays for dozens of development engineers waiting for critical feedback from their tests.

A huge negative consequence is that the excessive delays not only affect development schedules but also

Waiting for a Resource

According to queuing theory, the waiting time for a resource such as a central mainframe computer increases gradually as more of the resource is used. But when the utilization passes 70%, delays increase dramatically.

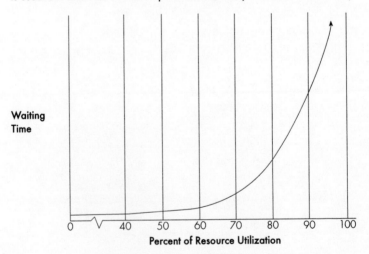

discourage people from experimenting, thus squelching their ability to innovate. So in the long term, running additional computer equipment at a lower utilization level might well be worth the investment. An alternative solution is to move those resources away from cost centers and under the control of developers, who have strong incentives for fast feedback.

The Benefits of Front-Loaded Development

IN THE 1990s, Toyota made a major push to accelerate its product development cycle. The objective was to shorten the time from the approval of a body style to the first retail sales, thereby increasing the likelihood that Toyota kept up with the rapidly changing tastes of consumers.

Toyota made a concerted effort to identify and solve design-related problems earlier in product development—a concept known as *front-loading*. To accomplish that, the company implemented a number of initiatives, such as involving more manufacturing engineers during the product-engineering stage, increasing the transfer of knowledge between projects, investing substantially in computer-aided design and engineering tools, and developing rapid-prototyping capabilities.

To measure the benefits of these initiatives—and to monitor the company's evolving capabilities for early problem solving—Toyota tracked problems over multiple development projects. (See the exhibit "Solving Problems Earlier.") The knowledge that a higher percentage of problems were being solved at earlier stages reassured

Solving Problems Earlier

As Toyota intensified its front-loading efforts, it was able to identify and solve problems much earlier in the development process.

In the early 1990s (see top graph), the first initiatives for front-loading began. Formal, systematic efforts to improve face-to-face communication and joint problem solving between the prototype shops and production engineers resulted in a higher relative percentage of problems found with the aid of first prototypes. Communication between different engineering sections (for instance, between body, engine, and electrical) also improved.

In the mid-1990's (see middle graph), the second front-loading initiatives called for three dimensional computer-aided design, resulting in a significant increase of problem identification and solving prior to stage 3 (first prototypes).

In the ongoing third front-loading initiatives (see bottom graph), Toyota is using computer-aided engineering to identify functional problems earlier in the development process, and the company is transferring problem and solution information from previous projects to the front end of new projects. As a result, Toyota expects to solve at least 80% of all problems by stage 2—that is, before the first prototypes are made. And because the second-generation prototypes (stage 5) are now less important to over-all problems solving, Toyota will be able to eliminate parts of that process, thereby further reducing time and cost without affecting product quality.

Toyota's managers that they could aggressively reduce both development time and cost without risking product quality. In particular, between the first and third front-loading initiatives, Toyota slashed the cost (including the number of full physical prototypes needed) and time of development by between 30% and 40%.

It should be noted that in the early 1990s Toyota substantially reorganized its development activities, resulting in more effective communication and coordination between the different groups. This change most likely

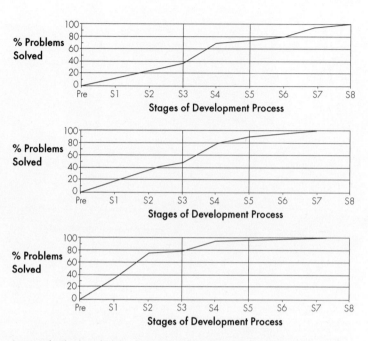

Source: Stefan Thomke and Takahiro Fujimoto, "The Effect of 'Front-Loading' Problem-Solving on Product Development Performance," *The Journal of Product Innovation Management,* Vol. 17, No. 2, March 2000.

accounted for some of the performance improvements observed, particularly during the first front-loading initiatives.

Originally published in February 2001
Reprint R0102D

About the Contributors

CLAYTON M. CHRISTENSEN is Professor of Business Administration at the Harvard Business School, with a joint appointment in the Technology Operations Management and General Management faculty groups. His research and teaching interests center on the management of technological innovation, developing organizational capabilities, and finding new markets for new technologies. Before joining the Harvard Business School faculty, Dr. Christensen served as Chairman and President of CPS Corporation, a firm he cofounded with several MIT professors in 1984. His writings have won several awards including the Production and Operations Management Society's 1991 William Abernathy Award, the Newcomen Society's award for the best paper in business history, the 1995 McKinsey Award for the best article published in the *Harvard Business Review*, and the 1997 Financial Times/Booz-Allen and Hamilton Global Business Book Award for his book, *The Innovator's Dilemma*.

ANDREW HARGADON is Assistant Professor in the Management Department at the Warrington College of Business Administration at the University of Florida. He received his Ph.D. from the Management Science and Engineering Department of Stanford University's School of Engineering, where he was the Boeing Fellow in Stanford's Alliance for Innovative Manufacturing. Prior to this, Professor Hargadon worked on designing new products for Apple Computer and IDEO Product Development. He also taught creative problem-solving in Stanford's Mechanical Engineering-Product Design Program. Professor Hargadon's research and teaching focuses on the management of technology and innovation. He has written on topics including knowledge management in new product development, creativity and innovation among engineers, speed and quality in new product development, and the role of design in the diffusion of innovation.

ROSABETH MOSS KANTER is an internationally known business leader, award-winning author, and expert on strategy, innovation, and the power to change. She is the Ernest L. Arbuckle Professor of Business Administration at the Harvard Business School and an advisor to major corporations and government entities worldwide. Her most recent book is *Evolve!: Succeeding in the Digital Culture of Tomorrow*. She is also the author of best-sellers including *Men and Women of the Corporation, The Change Masters, When Giants Learn to Dance,* and *World Class.* In 1997–1998, she conceived of and led the Business Leadership in the Social Sector (BLSS) project, involving more than 100 national leaders in dialogue about business-government partnerships to improve American communities. Before joining the Harvard Business School faculty in 1986, Kanter was a tenured professor at Yale University and a Fellow in Law and Social Science at Harvard Law School. She has served as Editor of the Harvard Business Review, and is cofounder of Goodmeasure, Inc., a consulting firm that develops leadership and consulting tools based on her work. Named one of the 100 most important women in America by the *Ladies Home Journal* and one of the 50 most powerful women in the world by the *London Times,* she has received nineteen honorary doctoral degrees and more than a dozen leadership awards. She serves on numerous national and civic boards including City Year, the national urban youth service corps.

W. CHAN KIM is the Boston Consulting Group Bruce D. Henderson Chair Professor of Strategy and International Management at INSEAD and Fellow of the World Economic Forum at Davos. Prior to joining INSEAD, he was Professor at the University of Michigan Business School. He has published numerous articles on strategy and managing the multinational in *Academy of Management Journal, Management Science, Organizational Science, Strategic Management Journal, Journal of International Business Studies, Sloan Management Review, Harvard Business Review,* and others. His writings have been featured in the *Wall Street Journal, The Financial Times,* the *New York Times, The Economist,* and *The International Herald Tribune.*

IAN MACMILLAN is Academic Director of the Sol C. Snider Entrepreneurial Research Center at The Wharton School, University of Pennsylvania. He is also the Fred Sullivan Professor of Entrepreneurship in the Management Department. Formerly, he was Director of the Entrepreneurship Center at New York University and a teacher at Columbia and Northwestern Universities and the University of South Africa. Prior to joining the academic world, Professor MacMillan was a chemical engineer and gained experience in gold and uranium mining, chemical and explosives manufacturing, oil refining, soap and food production, and the South African Atomic Energy Board. He has consulted to IBM, HP, Intel, Citibank, American Reinsurance, Sonera (Finland), Matsushitsa, Sumitomo, and Olymous (Japan), and LG Group (Korea) among others. Professor MacMillan's articles have appeared in numerous journals, including the *Harvard Business Review, Sloan Management Review, Journal of Business Venturing, Administrative Science*

Quarterly, Academy of Management Journal, Academy of Management Review, Academy of Management Executive, Management Science, and *Strategic Management Journal.* His most recent book, *The Entrepreneurial Mindset,* is coauthored with Rita Gunther McGrath.

RENÉE MAUBORGNE is the INSEAD Distinguished Fellow and Affiliate Professor of Strategy and Management at INSEAD and Fellow of the World Economic Forum at Davos. She is also President of ITM Research, a research group committed to discovering ideas that matter in the knowledge economy. She has published numerous articles on strategy and managing the multinational in *Academy of Management Journal, Management Science, Organization Science, Strategic Management Journal, Journal of International Business Studies, Sloan Management Review, Harvard Business Review,* and others. She is also a contributor to the *Wall Street Journal, The Financial Times,* the *New York Times, The Economist,* and *The International Herald Tribune.*

RITA GUNTHER MCGRATH is Associate Professor in the Management Division of the Columbia University Graduate School of Business. She received the Academy of Management Review Best Paper Award for her 1999 paper, "Falling Forward: Real Options Reasoning and Entrepreneurial Failure". She is also the recipient of the Entrepreneurship Theory and Practice Award for the best conceptual paper submitted to the 1996 and 1992 Academy of Management Meetings, as well as of the inaugural (1992) Kauffman Foundation Fellowship in Entrepreneurship. Prior to her life in academia, she managed major information technology projects, worked in the political arena, and founded two start-ups. In her research and consulting, she has worked with companies such as Hewlett-Packard, Intel, DuPont, Citigroup (formerly Citibank), Chubb & Son, Texas Instruments, Ericsson, Sonera, Inc., and many others. She is active in Columbia's executive education programs and is the Faculty Director for "Leading Entrepreneurial Change in Organizations." McGrath is the author of many book chapters and scholarly articles that have appeared in the *Harvard Business Review, Strategic Management Journal, Management Science, Academy of Management Review, Research-Technology Management,* and *Academy of Management Journal.* She serves on the editorial boards of the *Academy of Management Journal, Strategic Management Journal,* and *Journal of Business Venturing.*

One of Harvard Business School's first Dean's Research Fellows, MICHAEL OVERDORF worked with Professor Clayton Christensen to write and conduct research on the management processes and decision criteria that enable companies to effectively identify and manage disruptive innovations. He is currently Chairman and CEO of Innosight, a company he cofounded with Christensen to help companies improve their ability to manage innovation. Prior to his work at HBS, Mr. Overdorf worked for Alcoa where he held various managerial positions in operations and product development.

MARY SONNACK began her career at 3M Company thirty-three years ago as a laboratory chemist and is now Division Scientist at 3M Company, specializing in introducing and diffusing new product development processes throughout the company. During her tenure at 3M, she has held various positions in product development including laboratory manager for product development, process development, and the pilot plant. She was instrumental in bringing Quality Functional Deployment into 3M and has had a major role in forming a new business area within the company. Ms. Sonnack has taught managerial classes at the University of Minnesota and her career has been the subject of two MBA cases by the Harvard Business School. She spent the academic year of

1994–1995 as a Visiting Scholar at Massachusetts Institute of Technology, to work with Professor Eric von Hippel on a 3M sponsored project to diffuse the Lead User Method throughout the company. Recently, Harvard Business School wrote two MBA cases on the application of Lead User Research at 3M.

ROBERT I. SUTTON is Professor of Management Science and Engineering in the Stanford Engineering School, where he is codirector of the Center for Work, Technology, and Organization and an active researcher in the Stanford Technology Ventures Program. He is Professor of Organizational Behavior (by courtesy) at the Stanford Business School, and a Fellow at IDEO Product Development and at Reactivity. Dr. Sutton has served on the editorial boards of numerous scholarly publications, and currently serves as coeditor of *Research in Organizational Behavior*. He has published over 70 articles and chapters in scholarly and applied publications. Dr. Sutton's recent books include *The Knowing-Doing Gap: How Smart Firms Turn Knowledge Into Action*, coauthored with Jeffrey Pfeffer, and *Weird Ideas That Work: 11 1/2 Counterintuitive Ways to Spark and Sustain Innovation*, which will be published in Fall 2001.

STEFAN THOMKE, Associate Professor of Business Administration at Harvard Business School, has taught product development and operations management courses in the MBA Program and Executive Programs in several countries around the world. Having authored or coauthored more than three dozen articles, case studies and notes, Professor Thomke's research and publications focus on how companies can manage new technologies and process methodologies to achieve dramatic improvements in their product development performance. His writings have appeared in journals such as *California Management Review, Harvard Business Review, Journal of*

Product Innovation Management, Management Science, Research Policy, and *Scientific American.*

ERIC VON HIPPEL is Professor or Management of Technology and Entrepreneurship at Massachusetts Institute of Technology. His research focuses on breakthrough innovations and the increasingly important role of users in the innovation process. He has shown that "Lead Users" are the actual early development sites for many of the most commercially important innovations ranging from scientific instruments to the World Wide Web. Recently, Professor von Hippel has been exploring how to equip leading-edge users with "User Toolkits for Innovation" so that they can develop advanced new products or services within a design framework provided by an e-commerce or traditional company. A number of articles on these topics can be downloaded from the website leaduser.com.

Index